The Last Poets in New York City around 1969. Left to right: Abiodun Oyewole, Nilija, Jalal Mansur Nurridin, Umar Bin Hassan. (Courtesy of Michael Ochs Photo Archives)

On a Mission

The Last Poets in New York City around 1970. Left to right: Jalal, Nilija, Umar. (Courtesy of Michael Ochs Photo Archives)

THE LAST POETS

On a Mission

Selected Poems and
a History of The Last Poets

Abiodun Oyewole and Umar Bin Hassan
with Kim Green

An Owl Book
Henry Holt and Company
New York

Henry Holt and Company, Inc.
Publishers since 1866
115 West 18th Street
New York, New York 10011

Henry Holt® is a registered trademark of Henry Holt and Company, Inc.

Published in Canada by Fitzhenry & Whiteside Ltd.,
195 Allstate Parkway, Markham, Ontario L3R 4T8.

Library of Congress Cataloging-in-Publication Data
Oyewole, Abiodun.
On a mission: the last poets/Abiodun Oyewole and Umar Bin Hassan
with Kim Green
p.   cm.
"An Owl book."
I. Bin Hassan, Umar.   II. Green, Kim.   III. Title.
PS3565.Y3505   1996   96-25676
811'.54—dc20   CIP

ISBN 0-8050-4778-6

Henry Holt books are available for special promotions and premiums.
For details contact: Director, Special Markets.

First Edition—1996

Designed by James Sinclair

Printed in the United States of America
All first editions are printed on acid-free paper. ∞

1 3 5 7 9 10 8 6 4 2

Contents

• *This symbol is used to indicate a space between stanzas of a poem wherever such spaces are lost in pagination.*

Left to right: Umar, Amiri Baraka, Abiodun. (Courtesy of Risasi-Zachariah Dais)

Foreword

Abiodun and Umar are the most consistent carriers of the name The Last Poets. For the Knowers, we know the name once meant the great Gylan Kain, now in the Netherlands (as is traditional, for a time, for Orpheus) . . . David Nelson, now a minister in Colorado, and Felipe Luciano, my man, the courageous leader of the Young Lords, a funky warrior, like we usually is. And Abiodun, on the set, from the beginning.

The Abiodun LPs have established the most known sound and image of The Last Poets with Umar and Jalil. These LPs have created a popular oeuvre that speaks and will speak from us, through them, to the world.

The rhythmic animation of word, poem, image, as word-music, is the Djali. This form came out of the revolutionary sixties' Black Arts movement, from way back beyond sorrow songs and chattel wails. Where we created the word as living music, raising it off the still, Apollonian, alabaster page. Now the words become a score. Like Duke's (we wish) to be lifted off the page, like a composition needing to be musicked, by the Djali, to fully live.

"Performance" poetry, the dead people said, to claim a grandness, by inference, for the dead academic, earless, soul sold emptiness of that verse championed by the Beast who is a man! For the Beast loves only death. Only robbery and murder permit this Beast to live. The Last Poets take life and give it back live to the living. They remember themselves through the souls of Black folks, alive these many centuries, we are slow to anger. Our art describes our past, the middle passage, Slavery, the struggle of the Afro-American Nation! For Democracy, Self-Determination, and the destruction of national oppression and capitalism.

Abiodun and Umar are like a bubbling rhythm spoken out of what the streets themselves can hear. The sixties' Black Arts movement, which sought, and still seeks, to create a revolutionary, self-reliant art to transform ourselves, as a revolutionary culture, which at full strength and consciousness to overthrow "White America" (the fascist media abstraction) like the Brown Bomber wasted Schmeling. Oh, yes—It's coming, sure as the world, not even by ourselves, but with all those willing to be human beings, no matter their nationality, it is their ideology and acts that define the living from the soon to be dead. "Whose side you're on," as my wife, Amina, says.

"I Rise in Fire"! Yes, it is a prophecy, The Black Bird is prophet against the Devil's profit. The Soul of Blackness sings, chants, even wiggles after a touchdown the ghosts couldn't stop.

The power of the Djali of the sixties, Black Arts movement, returns, Oh, Charlie, you hip thang, as Rap, old word, the beat on the wood. The "Log" in which we keep notes (Blue) on reality and history and who am we us i—was is and will be.

The Last Poets are the prototype Rappers, the transmitters of the mass poetry style of the Black Arts sixties, through the whatever of WA and ourselves inside wailing for light, with the hard rhythms of What Is brought into the Now. A Jazz-linked rhythm and Blues feeling the Rappers copped forms a direct connection with content (till the Dangs got in it)!

The Last Poets speak, in the tradition, from Fred to Margaret to Trane, of our real lives. The beat, the feeling, form and content come from there. From the here we hear and see. Our rising I. It is the Is Story. The seed. The scene. It is teaching, because it is true not just "propaganda," which could be a lie.

The Last Poets' message of self-wisdom is Black, is the living history of our consciousness. And who is not "Black," as a historic confirmation of the truth of Civilization's origin? That humanity will prevail, and civilization begin. That the heinous crime of slavery is like the moth wasted by the flame, a teacher said, "You did it to yourself, Krishna!"

The Last Poets are in the tradition of Revolutionary Art for Cultural Revolution. The razor. And certainly, Hey, Now, a lotta peepas know, "them negroes carry razors." Or perhaps, for The Last Poets, their razor is a *raiser,* Revolutionary Art for Cultural Revolution. Oh, yes, Freedom is our aesthetic and social and political quest. "FREEDOM!" we say. We think it is good, we think it is beautiful.

The Last Poets sing and chant and speak to us—they say, "Ba, Ba, Black Sheep—You got the wool!" That's the "Mission" they on, and been on, to arm us with true self-consciousness. They say, "Come together to create life . . . love . . . to create create."

They say we are . . . "afraid of revolution." They say our minds are, "in a state of mental paralysis," "all the while our children are dying . . . all the while, a fucking ghost is killing us . . ." Yes, they say, now it is the Will, the fuel of the future. Who loves the world of animal cannibal is both and The Last Poets are remembering and re-creating the science. Yet, like most of us they have to judge themselves and ourselves again and again to re-re-understand that it is a not a color or a religion or a nationality killing us, it is a social economic system, and our collaboration, conscious or un, that allows this humiliation and pain. Understanding, creating, re-creating, remembering, the science, yes, the "magic words," actually, formulas, to waste you, Dr. Dracula.

These are the chants of the creating of the New that comes twisting in struggle with the old. The rational mind of what is coming into existence, at war with what is going out of existence, and hence, irrational. Ah, such beauty, is a rhythm, a song. A formula of what is the science of Beast Killing. For who would slay the Beast must study and learn and understand and then be inspired by the fire of all that will live. For who cannot hate, cannot love . . . who cannot kill, cannot protect life! (To paraphrase the great Chinese Djali, Lu Shun.)

In the tradition of democracy of revolution. In the spirit of Afro America. As creative rise in, who must create a new world, out of fire and like our Ptah Baby selves, rise again, with as Art, existence created by consciousness and science. The greatest truth is that which exists always! Art that speaks for the people and to them, functional as lists of things to think and do, things you thought and hate to think about. The Last Poets wants "Nigguhs" to stop bullshitting and hoping God is America, still disguised as the Devil. They urge us to be self-conscious and dig The Beast in The West, and the Easternness and Africanness, the niggers uptight, hard as slavery still maintains.

The Last Poets speak as outrage, as the persona of the hip the slick the knowledge speak, the nationalist, the Afrocentric, the patriotic and militant traditional Bigger resistance-type nigger. Like Sonny's Son (Bubadika's Lumumba) describes, "I'm the kina nigger you don never wanna meet!"

They speak to the necessity of united militant self as defiance, resistance, the magic of "will" as creative elaboration of the living. The Rappers have confirmed that the word is still the power of what it brings. And that our Art is a weapon of our struggle, as anyone's art also relays their minds and feelings, their vision and their direction. And if we understand that art and literary criticism are a form of class (hence, national) struggle, then we should understand that until the revolutionary artists create their own superstructure, their own organizations, networks, institutions, to criticize, encourage, distribute, and teach, we are in a razor fight without a razor.

Say this to point out that the Word Music we make, Poetry-Jazz, Rap, is a sharp weapon needing to be held in our own hands and kept sharp and pointed at the enemy (not at our sisters and wives and mothers). It is time we rallied our troops and began the mobilization of the mouths and the hearts and the brains and the souls. For we must understand what Fred D. and Mao TT meant when they said, "Find out the exact amount of injustice any people accept, and you will find out the exact amount of injustice they receive" and "Cast Aside Illusion, Prepare to Struggle!"

All these ferocious revolutionary wordships and Djali, we got, must be got together, you know. Let the Revolutionary Festivals and Conferences and Mobilizations of us begin. Or re-begin. If the word is to be given, let us gather the revolutionaries of the word-music, The Last Poets, and Kain, Nelson, Luciano, Jayne Cortez her Firespitters, Amina and My Blue Ark, Sekou Sundiata, Gaston Neal, Linton Kwesi Johnson, Mutabaruka, Kalamu ya Salaam, Askia Toure, John Sinclair, Louis Rivera, Sonia, Haki, Little Willie K. from South Africa and Duma, Sterling P, yall know . . . Pedro Pietri, Sandra Esteves, Miguel and the Nuyoricans, Cheryl Byron, the young folks, Ras & Willie Perdomo, Tony Medina, all those who can run the revolutionary line with hot musicked words. The D.C. oralutionaries, they in LA and Chicago, New Orleans and St. Louis, the everywhere we is, they. I mean all who got the word on fire loaded in the mind and heart, with the soul of the sun, we children of Africa and Pan America, let us get the army together, and begin to create a superstructure, a mass mind of revolution. So, sampling Mao again, "Let A Hundred Flowers Bloom, Let A Hundred Schools of Thought Contend!"

Yes, like the Charlie Bird sang, as we-us-i rose straight up, us tale on fire, smoking like blue laser gone, "Now's The Time! Now's The Time!" we wailed, and the chorus, "I Rise In Fire!"

March, 1996
Amiri Baraka

Acknowledgments

Umar:

There are people to be thanked on this journey. First of all, my Lord and protector Allah to whom all praises are due. My grandmother, mother, and sister Sandra. Bill Laswell for having enough courage or game to take a chance on me. Without *Be Bop or Be Dead* there would be no second coming of The Last Poets. Abiodun for his patience and understanding. The partnership has had its ups and downs, only natural for two men of our passion and egos, but we've done it and we've done it together. Thanks, Dun. Babatunde, thank you, big brother, for your balance and strength. We couldn't have done it without you. To all my children and their mothers for that hidden source of inspiration. To Pharoah and Asante for keeping me musically tuned. To Ms. Estina Baker for keeping my imagination near the edge. To Ace for the wonderful conversations. To Jonathan and Maurice for giving The Last Poets play in the beginning of the second coming. To Roberta Magrini for her wonderful pasta and helping hand on *Be Bop or Be Dead.* To Rhyme and Reason. Trish. Keisha. Miss Charlotte and the indefatigable and undeniable Bill Adler. Thanks for helping put The Last Poets back on the scene. To Carolyn Sachs and Carolyn Master, our management team. Your work, your very hard work, has been appreciated. You have been very important. To Henry Holt for being so daring, especially Greg Hamlin. To Ms. Kim Green, one of the sharpest minds I've encountered on any person, anywhere, in a long time! Thank you.

And to my homegirl Tracy Sherrod, thank you, baby girl! I'm going to take you up on those grits and gravy sooner or later. To Phil Asbury, a true counselor in the truest sense of the word. Thanx, Phil. To all our fans, loyal and contemplating, thank you for your support. To my father, Sonny Huling, who left me with all this sensitivity, creativity, and imagination. And to those whom I forgot, thank you, too! And finally one big special thank you to one person who has made this all possible, myself. I love you, Umar Bin Hassan. Thank you, baby boy, The victory is yours, if you want it.

Dun:

First and foremost I'd like to acknowledge the spiritual force that governs my life and bestows blessings upon me continuously. In addition, I'd like to acknowledge: Mother, Daddy Joe, Grandaddy, Mommy; my brothers, Abdul Raheemhaqq and Cornell; my sisters, Anita and Janice; my children, Pharoah, Aina, Obadele, Ebon, and Suwande; their mothers, Olubiji, Nayo, Ayisha, and Pepsi; all my in-laws, my friends, nieces and nephews, aunts, uncles, and cousins (Cincinnati crew). A special acknowledgment to Ace for keeping the fire burning. Acknowledgment to all of The Last Poets: David, Kain, Felipe, Suliaman, Jalal, Nilijah, Babatunde, and Umar.

Acknowledgment to the hip-hop generation, the new nineties poets, the next generation of jazz musicians, and to every living soul that cares about the well-being of every living thing. Let your light shine.

Kim:

Thank you to the Spirit for the skill and the patience it takes to write. Thank you, Jaime, for always understanding, always caring, and watching out, and always helping me laugh at the things that seem so bad before you put your magical wisdom on them. I love you more every day. Daddy, thank you for all the Sunday rides to "the book." And thank you for your undying pride in me and devotion to me. Thank you, Tracy Sherrod, for your beautiful faith in my ability. To all of my family, near and far, thank you for always expecting me to do big things. I am lucky to have such faith behind me. Dun, thank you for always being warm, supportive, and honest. Umar, thank you for your hard-won respect and for being a true lesson in determination. Thank you Carolyn Sachs for listening to my— well . . . you know. Thank you to The Last Poets for honoring me with your trust and your most important work. Peace and love.

Introduction

I have taken on a heavy load: to document the undocumented history of The Last Poets with nothing to go on and nothing to go by, except the words of two of the original seven members, and the weight of all their hopes and dreams.

Anyone who knows Abiodun Oyewole and Umar Bin Hassan will tell you that they are a trip. I was told, but I didn't take it as seriously as I should have. They *are* a trip, but not in the clichéd sense of the word. They are a virtual journey back in time and to the core of the Black revolutionary experience in America.

From the start of this project, I felt something menacing and mysterious about The Last Poets. Their history came to me in scraps of old clippings that appeared in obscure fanzines around the world. Although all the stories conflicted and featured different poets, the common denominator was the passion that every writer had for the words of The Last Poets. Passion and love are two key words for The Last Poets, I discovered.

When this project came to me, I went to the library to find the past books on The Last Poets. There were none. "There are none?" I asked. Nope, just *Vibes From the Scribes,* a flimsy poetry collection of, again, only two poets: Jalal Nuriddin and Suliaman El Hadi. No history, no information, and no real mention of the missing five Poets. I couldn't understand why there was nothing on them. I couldn't believe no one had taken the time to go beyond their brilliant words to find out about the men themselves and how they came to call themselves The Last Poets. After all, these are the men that gave Black people back their own possibilities by stressing the idea of revolution.

Now that I've attempted to piece the puzzle together, it is easy to see why no one else has. The story of The Last Poets is muddled and confused. There are a lot of players, a lot of versions, so that it is hard to get to the truth. Just for the history books, I give you these facts: The Last Poets were born on May 19, 1968, in Marcus Garvey Park (aka Mt. Morris Park) at a celebration for Malcolm X's birthday. The original seven members are: David Nelson, Gylan Kain, Abiodun Oyewole, Felipe Luciano, Umar Bin Hassan, Jalal Nurridin, and Suliaman El Hadi. And, no, Gil Scott Heron was never one of them.

The other absolute truth about The Last Poets is that, yes, from their minds came the classic poems "Niggers Are Scared of Revolution," "When The Revolution Comes," "This Is Madness," and many, many, many more.

The Last Poets' story is of seven passionate young men in search of love—not from women—but simple love of self. It is seven men who decided they couldn't put up with what the world was dishing out and were willing to risk it all to make a change. These men met each other while all were on a mission to bring change with truth. The mission was also to revolutionize the way people looked at themselves.

What they didn't know about was the venom that fame and success carry. What they didn't know was that greed and fear and insecurity can turn men into animals, brothers into strangers, and partners into enemies. They didn't know that passion is stronger than love—and more dangerous.

Each Last Poet tells a different version of the group's story, with different heroes and different villains, yet the moral is the same: Being a Last Poet was their lifeline; it gave them purpose and meaning on this earth. No mortal can decipher it. No one can make sense of it, because it is not clear even to them.

When I met Abiodun and Umar, I immediately fell in love with them. Abiodun is tall and boisterous, with a smile that lasts all day and a cavernous laugh that warms you from head to toe. Umar is deep, dark, and quiet. He didn't speak to me much the first night (or the second for that matter), but he acknowledged me because I am a Scorpio, like him. He referred to me simply as "Scorpio" all night and I knew that, for him, that was a lot.

Of all the sections of this book, this introduction has been the most difficult for us all to agree on. Naively, I thought I was going to make it all clear; tell the story as it was told to me, with my own little twist. I didn't realize the impossibility of trying to make sense of lives that haven't made sense of themselves. I didn't see that you can't impose logic on the highly emotional lives of seven men caught up in a passion and swept away with the tide.

In my opinion, The Last Poets' story teaches what America does to its Black men. The Last Poets' story teaches Black men what they do to each other. And, lastly, The Last Poets' poems teach us why.

What The Last Poets want you to get out of their story is that after all the negative, came the positive. After arrests, drug addictions, fighting, name-calling, and feuding, there is still an incredible body of work that will immortalize them. After all those things they are all fathers and leaders in their communities. And after all that, they are still The Last Poets.

When I first started interviewing and outlining the book, Umar doubted me. He thought I was too "middle class" for this exercise in revolutionary righteousness. Umar thought I didn't know enough about struggle or Black folks. I was indignant that they would feel that I, Black, a woman, a writer juggling a freelance career and a job in *corporate America,* couldn't understand their rage.

The early interview sessions were smooth. Both Dun and Umar were generous with information and anecdotes. They were animated, funny, sorrowful, and entertaining. The stories of the past were peppered with names: David Nelson, Jalal, Suliaman, Felipe, and Gylan Kain. Sometimes they were mentioned in reference to their genius, and other days these names were hissed and spat.

I asked once if it would be possible for me to reach any of the other Poets and was met with rolled eyes, polite laughter, and skepticism. Finally, Dun said, "You can call David. Here's his number."

I called David Nelson a few days later and explained who I was and what I was doing. David, now a minister in North Carolina, turned sour when he heard "The Last Poets" fall from my mouth. "Who are you again, Miss Green? What makes you an authority on The Last Poets? What do you even know about them? Where did they get their name?"

I fumbled to regurgitate what Dun had told me the night before: "The Last Poets' name was inspired by a poem by Willie Kgositsile, which used the phrase 'The Last Poets'."

"Wrong," he interrupted. "The name was put in *my* head by God. See, your book will not have integrity," he scolded. "You don't know what you're talking about. You can't tell the story after only speaking to Umar and Dun."

"Well, how can I contact the others?" I asked.

"Well, Felipe probably won't speak to you, but you can try to call him. He's already told me negative things about you and this book," David said.

David and I spoke for a while longer. He stressed the importance of a healing between the Poets. He wants more than anything to see the group have a reunion and to get over "this thing." He's frustrated by it and out of answers. David is optimistic, thinking that all the members want to fix it, despite the fact that no one has ever made a real effort in several years.

I was disappointed to hear that these men who should be my idols were in a thirty-year-old argument over rights and who wrote what. How could such things ever have gotten confused in the first place? David assured me that this book could help the healing. He urged me to write the book with that in mind.

David went on to say that the book wouldn't be complete without me interviewing and including all of the children of The Last Poets.

("Do you know how many children that is?") He insisted that they are living legends and revolutionaries by bloodline. I was sad when I finished speaking with David. He seemed to be living in a dream of what The Last Poets could have been, but weren't.

Nevertheless, I was moved by him. I wanted to help ease the feud with this book, but didn't know how. I tried to call Felipe Luciano (now a newscaster in New York). He didn't return my call.

I called Dun. I told him what happened with David. He laughed. He laughed in that fatherly way of his that makes everything immediately okay. He told me to forget it. Just keep going. So I did.

I decided that the way to make David, Dun, Umar, and myself happy was to be brutally honest. Paint the picture. Break it down. I hoped that when the Poets read it in their own private moments, they'd see their own chaos and want to rectify it. I do believe in the power of words.

The original introduction was political. It was harsh, I admit, but I was passionate about the implications of this. I was angry at what happened to these seven talented men who had, since their beginning, fought in the street, stolen from each other, turned on each other, and worse. I was angry that that always happens when success gets into the mix. Seemingly, a lot more often to Black people.

I was feeling my oats as a writer. I was secretly pleased that I understood it all so well. I explained away all the "indiscretions" of the Poets by putting them into a category with other "fallen" Black figures. I put them in the league of other people who have been made an example of. I named Huey Newton, Michael Jackson, Marion Berry, Billie Holiday, Tupac Shakur, James Brown, Clarence Thomas, Mike Tyson, and Magic Johnson. I also mentioned that there are too many to mention.

I tried to give them all dignity by saying that their weaknesses and flaws may be inherent to Blacks in America, as they often succumb to the pressures of racism. I wrote:

After all, being in the dark is what *Black-in-America-ness* is all about. To let go of that, to dig deep, to be forgiving, to be selfless, to be sharing would be going against the very culture that we've inherited from our slave masters. To be those things would be a return to our African selves. America won't want that. America won't have it.

When I came up for air after furiously writing all of this down, I called Dun. I was starving for his opinion. He was delighted. He told me that I *got* it. "That was deep," he said after I read him a portion. He simply said, "Don't forget our positive aspects." Oh, no, I was just getting started, the last seven pages were the pages that brought this piece into the light. I spoke of the significance of the work and these experiences. I named all the things that would signal that the Poets had risen above this calamity. I talked about Dun's educational achievements, his teaching posts, and the success of his children. For Umar, I mentioned what a great father he was and how he was a mentor to many young struggling poets. These are all the things they need for you to know. When I finished the introduction, of which I was very proud, I sent it to them. They were not pleased. They hated it, in fact.

It was all a blur after that. Next thing I knew, Dun and Umar were in my office yelling, cursing, and telling me that I wasn't imaginative. They said that I was too negative and too dark, when really what I had written had been the truth. *The truth hurts.* And just like the poison tendency of their pens, they couldn't take the poison of mine. *Niggers are scared of revolution.*

"Absolutely not," I was told. "This won't do." "Back to the drawing board." "Rewrite it." "Talk about the positives." "There's no hope in what you've written." I disagreed. "It's too dark." I disagreed. "It's too negative." I disagreed. "You called me old!" said Dun. And I had, in the context that young men who otherwise might have thought him "old" have a lot of respect for him and his work.

"But what about the *significance* of the negative things?" I argued. "Use your imagination," they told me. "Tell the negative, but don't make it seem negative." Umar was really disappointed in me. He didn't say much that day. He sighed and shook his head a lot. I was heartbroken. There's nothing more scathing than a Scorpio-on-Scorpio attack. He was questioning my sting, and using his on me. After the argument I had lost my will to fight for what I believed, which is what happened to the *collective* Last Poets.

This group is an example of an important phenomenon in America that makes our leaders fall beneath the pressure of getting theirs in a country that is so insincere in its giving to people of color. The Last Poets show that we all collectively and individually must rise up. And when put to the task, we often do.

The second introduction was benign. I wrote what they wanted. A discussion of just how great they were. And, make no mistake, they *are* great. I wrote:

The Last Poets' mission was to pull the people up out of the rubble of their lives. These courageous, articulate, artistic scribes knew, deep down, that poetry could save the people. They knew that if Black people could see and hear themselves and their struggles through the spoken word, that they would be moved to change. They knew that if they took a stand for Black people and exposed their deepest fears and fires, that America could ignore them no more.

It was a twenty-page Hallmark card. Umar and Dun loved this version. They raved. They told me I was a poet. Practically the first honorary female Last Poet. I was relieved, but deep inside I felt a nagging that said it's still not right. I confidently rushed the new introduction to Tracy, our editor, who was not pleased. She hated it, in fact. She handed it back to me to rework. I couldn't face it again. I stalled.

A couple of weeks later Umar was stabbed in the throat by Jalal in Paris. He had to have an emergency tracheotomy. He ended up staying in a hospital in London for weeks.

Jalal? They hadn't heard from Jalal in years. What was he doing in Paris (where Umar was backstage preparing for a performance)? We all thought Jalal was in Brooklyn. It was a shock. How could anyone hurt Umar? Umar was the powerful one. The one who could do the hurting, not be hurt. Umar is so comfortable in his anger that his anger is his pride. I was scared that there was a possibility that some-one could be more intense, more enraged, and more proud than Umar. *Jalal.*

Jalal, the man who wrote, "Wake Up Niggers." Jalal, who Dun had once joked, he would kill if he darkened his doorstep. Jalal, the one Dun said would have to have his ass kicked before he could even have a discussion with him. Jalal, whom they also called a genius.

Dun was angry at Jalal because he's felt (for all these years) that Jalal had "disrespected" him. *Just like the kid who shoots his homey over a girl, a sneaker, or a sideward glance.* Disrespect is a key word to the Black man in America. It makes the Black man's blood boil.

The stabbing was a crime of passion. But unlike most crimes of passion, this one has resolution. As Umar recuperates, Dun still walks to the stage and does the gigs. He has a new clarity about The Last Poets now. He talks about the stabbing at each show. And, he tells the truth. At one show, he even performed with, yes, David Nelson. And, the rest of the Poets are now calling each other. *Crisis brings people together.* They have plans. They will work together, they may write together.

The feud may well be over, but it was real. Blood had to be spilled to anoint the ones that went before. The other Black men who've harmed each other in blinding rage and had nowhere else to aim their pain except at each other. Yes, *this is madness,* but it is reality too.

Well, I think, hope, and pray that my mission is over. I have introduced you to The Last Poets in the best way I know how: truthfully, honestly, and how I lived them. Now, let their mission begin. The mission is to enlighten you with poems that give Black people roots, purpose, and a beginning other than slavery and shame. These poems dare to put the crowns back on our heads and the grass beneath our feet.

Kim Green

On a Mission

Abiodun Oyewole, 1993. (Courtesy of Thi-Linh Le)

ABIODUN OYEWOLE
PERSONAL STATEMENT

The poetry began in me when I would ride through Harlem with my family and see Malcolm X speaking to people. I knew it was Malcolm only because my aunt pointed him out to me. I never saw him up close, but I'd see his orange head. His hair was outstanding. There was a certain glow about it, although I really don't want to say *glow*. I think it was his reddish hair and height that struck me the most. It seemed even redder when my aunt told me, "That man is going to get killed cause he's telling the truth."

May 19th, 1968, was the day that David Nelson, Gylan Kain, and I were going to read a poem in Mount Morris Park. We were participating in a celebration in memory of Malcolm X's life. David and I had both been writing love poems. A couple of his poems were about the

Civil Rights movement and things like that. I did have one political poem because Martin Luther King, Jr., had just gotten killed April 4th, and I wrote a poem about it called "Wall Street Journal." The piece talked about how people were going to capitalize off his death by making buttons, pins, posters, and pictures and sell them for $5. I thought I was just writing, and not only did it happen then, it has happened every year, since.

For this celebration, I knew I didn't have anything to read. I only had a poem that I had just written at Manhattan Community College. There was this sister at the college who actually worked in the library. She was about a year or two older than me, and I was trying to hang out with her. We had been going out but she had been giving me some grief. I wrote this verse:

> She's a rose with many thorns tearing pride out of my heart
> Though she blossoms in many forms her thorns remain always sharp.
> She rips, she hurts, yet stays projecting seductively, fragrant perfume.
> I protest in so many ways but my manhood she somehow consumes
> I'm torn between love and masculinity. The latter I need the most
> Her life from mine a separate entity
> I'm a man, this I cannot boast
> She more woman, than I a man
> Knows not her place by me, she thinks me a cactus withering in sand
>   closing her ears to my plea
> Let me free to roam in your garden, let me free to pride in your
>   perfume
> for the love I feel will soon be pardoned by the manhood
> I must quickly resume.

I remember this professor asked to see it. She said, "Wow, you're very good." That was the first time I think I had anyone ever read any of my things for any kind of critical appraisal or whatever. I really wasn't trying to be a poet. I was writing cause it felt right.

But now this day had come. I only knew a little about Harlem from Sundays with my Aunt Baby, so I was nervous. I did know about the movement; I read about it in the paper and I was watching it on TV.

All that was important was, Martin was dead—the movement was getting even more outrageous and riots were starting. Malcolm's legacy was building, because maybe we were starting to believe we needed to think more like Malcolm.

But for that day, I still didn't have anything to read, and I knew the Harlem crowd was rough. I knew I couldn't read "Emancipation." Not in Harlem. *"She's a rose with many thorns,"* my ass. I'd be runnin out of there with thorns in my ass for days. That'd be the end of my poetry and everything. So what I did in preparation was go to Harlem. I started walking around, just checking people out. I hung around and picked up one of the expressions of the time. "What is your thing?" was what everybody was saying. It meant What are you doing for the revolution? What are doing for the movement? Sometimes the answer was "Oh, I make bombs for the Panthers." Everybody had to have a thing. The Isley Brothers capitalized on this saying with the song: "It's Your Thing."

My poem, "What Is Your Thing?" was inspired by this saying. It was the first poem I read as a Last Poet. I'll never read that damn thing again because I lost it, and because now it seems irrelevant and stuck in that time frame. It's based on a colloquialism that is out of style. It was actually a shallow piece, in terms of not having the guts poetry should have.

It went something like:

What is your thing brother? Is it a Black thing? Will it save all Black women and children? Will it make Black children love Black people? Will it make Black people love Black children? Will it bring love into our communities?

This poem is not like "Two Little Boys" or "New York New York the Big Apple." I began to develop my style and skill after those pieces. "What Is Your Thing?" was strictly style and got me over in a crunch.

Kain's poem, on the other hand, was awesome. Without question, it was a masterpiece. It was one of the greatest poems I've ever read about niggers. It is the only poem that really defined niggers for me, ever. I remember it off the top of my head:

> Sweet, sweet puddin pie, Jesus, you brought me out from the midnight hour. You planted me in the light of day. You told me my yolk would be easy Lord. You told me my burdens would be light, but sometimes my cross gets heavy Lord. Sometimes my body starts to break. Pity me Lord that I might press on. Pity me Lord that I might press on. I heard God cry back after belching. After scratching his ass. Any sympathy I might have for you is somewhere between shit and sift. Hey niggers, dig yourselves, check yourselves, know who hell is yourself, who you are, what you are, where you are, know, niggers are very untogether people.

I know that poem probably better than I know my own. David's poem was "Are You Ready Black People?" It went: *Are you ready Black people, are you ready to build the world for Black women and children. Are you ready Black man. etc.* . . . It was a slogan piece, too, but it got a little more poetic because David had skills, and he merged his romantic stuff with his political stuff. He had a better handle on that than I felt that I did.

That was the beginning of The Last Poets. Gylan Kain, David Nelson, and myself. We met in David's house, we came onstage chanting a chant from Howard University's 1968 student demonstration: "Are you ready niggers, you got to be ready, are you ready niggers, you got to be ready." By the time we were all onstage everybody in the park was chanting it. There were drummers on the stage, too. We told them to play underneath us.

Following the success of that performance, we had auditions for percussionists. We also got a place called the East Wind. We had different people come through, including Nilija. I guess we chose him because his drumming was the most lyrical. He was talking back to us, he was communicating with us, and keeping the rhythm at the same time. His touch, his hands, were like a tongue.

At the time, the Black Panthers were big. The Black Panthers in New York City were very loyal to The Last Poets. They loved us, we loved them. Zayde Shakur was my personal bodyguard during the takeover of the site. Anywhere I needed to go, he was with me. I had some great Panther friends. Although our philosophies were different (the Poets weren't into the Communist thing), the strong chord between The Last Poets and the Black Panthers was our Nationalistic point of view. The desire for a unified Black front inspired many of the Black Panthers to poetry, too.

There was one poet Panther brother whose name should always be remembered: Kwesi Balagoon. He wrote a monster poem, "Wouldn't They Be Better Off." It was about loving white people, and seeing how much they're suffering. They can't stand the sun; they got those soggy eyes. Don't you think they'd be better off dead? Wouldn't you rather see them better off? He just runs his whole point like that. Like they're really only good if they're dead. It was a bold poem at that time. It was without any kind of remorse whatsoever. Balagoon got killed during the Black Liberation Army uprising.

Joanne Chesimard, who is now known as Assata Shakur, was living in Cuba. She was a sister who was very close to us—loyal and help-ful—and she was a Panther. We had a very wonderful relationship with the Panthers. They used to have us perform at quite a number of functions that they sponsored and we often had their poets perform at the East Wind.

The Last Poets ran into internal problems when we realized we all had a different vision of what we were supposed to be. At the time, Miles Davis was the perfect icon of a black celebrity. He was respected for his rawness and talent. Some of The Last Poets had aspirations to become celebrities like Miles. I was like, fuck that. My emotions were explosive.

5

I guess a lot of these feelings had been building up over time. I think anything at that moment in time might have blown me up. I wasn't happy being a poet. I began to feel that being a poet was a pitiful example of being a revolutionary. So, you write a poem, you get up onstage and you say it, you're a revolutionary. Wow, I mean come on, give me a break. Especially when somebody down the block just fed about ten kids with food stamps. Come on. Give me a break, there's more to do here. So, I decided to do more. I joined the Harlem Committee for Self-Defense, which was one of the many offshoots of the Black Panthers. My association with them led to the cops harassing me and caused me to leave New York City. I left tired of violence and fear, and fled to North Carolina, where I got deep into Afrocentricism and African culture.

I also went to Shaw University and did some teaching, organized a group called the Yoruba Society, and helped support Oyotunji, the village in South Carolina. I'm an original investor, along with the king of the village. I started a Yoruba Society at Shaw that sent a lot of Shaw students to the village. Today, a lot of students go there to trade in their American names for African names, get married, or to join the Yoruba religion. In fact, one of my students is now second in charge of the village. The village is in Sheldon, South Carolina. It's been around for about twenty-five years. I think it's at the top of the list for tourist attractions in South Carolina—it's known. Every magazine has written about it, including *Newsweek*.

When The Last Poets were touring in the summer of '95, we stopped in Oyotunji. The village needs some refurbishing, but it's still intact. People who are trying to get an understanding of their African self should definitely go through there.

While I was in the South, I became more involved in revolutionary activities. I took some money from the Watkins brothers, who were members of the grand dragons of the Ku Klux Klan in Knightdale, North Carolina. I knew from a kid in Students for a Democratic Society that these folks were Klanspeople and owned everything.

SDS was a radical white group that existed in the '60s. A short while before my arrest, there was a demonstration—the Klanspeople and the SDS were protesting against each other. I saw that there were quite a few liberal white folks involved in the Civil Rights movement. I was there because it was a demonstration and somebody had said some of the Klan members were going to march. And they did. They had on hoods and everything. It blew my mind.

The reason I went to prison was for taking money from the Watkins brothers. It started with taking guns though. Some of my brothers from the Yoruba Society took some guns, from the two gun shops in town; Thorn's and Dixie's. I designed the plan for the brothers in our organization to steal the guns because I had been challenged by some members of the organization to do so. They egged me on by saying a cultural revolutionary was weak. I had gotten a reputation, because till then I had not participated in anything risky. I was just known for philosophizing and being eloquently angry. The joke was: If the Man rolled up on you and decided to smack your woman around and shoot you, do you have a bulletproof dashiki? Or can you knock him out with your afro?

I had begun to be a target for these jokes. At one particular village meeting, this brother in my organization challenged me again, saying I wasn't militant enough and we need to have some military defense. I responded, "Any faggot can get a gun." What did I say that for? I had to go get some guns, or else I'm a "faggot." I designed a little plan and we took off Thorn's and Dixie's.

We took some serious ammunition and hid the guns in Meserve Hall, the basement of Shaw University's president's mansion. Although President King Cheek didn't know anything about this, we had access to the basement because it was the office for Shaw University's newspaper. I had fellahs in my group who had access to that section of the school. One group of guys dropped their duffel bag full of guns; thinking they heard some noises, they got scared and ran.

When the "scaredy cats" came back to find that the other brothers were successful, they went back to retrieve their guns. They got busted and got thrown in jail. The next morning, I was not around when the guns were brought in. I had to be invisible, because people would automatically think that I was the one that had done it, since I was known for being vocal. It ended up that I came on campus early in the morning anxious to see what had happened.

The coach of the football team stopped me: "Yo, Dun, some of your boys in jail." They were caught by cops at four in the morning riding around with one of the guns, the price tag still on it, in the damn trunk of the car.

One of the guys was supposed to be watching out, but he ended up to be working for the police. At first it was really unfathomable to comprehend his betrayal, even though we knew that type of thing happened. It just seemed so weird, cause we were kind of close, we trusted everybody.

After two of the brothers involved in the job were put in jail, the big-time revolutionaries began calling up mothers and fathers to get bail money. One of them happened to be the big-mouth brother who recited the whole scam from the beginning to the police. Bub was his nickname; I don't know his last name. Bub was crazy. Anyway, a likable brother, but just a little off. I wanted to get him out because I knew that he and his boy Marshall had extradition papers on their asses up in Pittsburgh, where they were from.

King Cheek told me he was going to get them out, but he didn't. He went to Detroit on some other business on behalf of a Shaw College connection there. In the meantime, the brothers remained in jail, when all he had to do was get a bail bondsman and vouch. I felt the responsibility of getting them out rested on my shoulders.

I used the information that I got from the kid at SDS. Me and my partner Alexander Young, who was the only brother I could really trust, had to have a lot of guts. The cops came on campus to retrieve the guns right away. They had to get permission first, since Shaw is a private campus. While they were doing so, we took a lot of the guns and spread them amongst ourselves. When the cops arrived, there were a few left. Later that day, I said to Alex, "Well listen, you got a gun, I got a gun, let's go get some money."

That was when we did the takeover—the robbery. It was a very interesting situation. The robbery was totally out of character for anything I had ever done. Straight up. There was a long manhunt afterward. However, we were seen by a sister and she ultimately picked us out in a line up. We both ended up getting 12–20 years.

As dark and as dreary and as wild and as bad as it might have seemed at the time, jail was a blessing. Jail wasn't so cool, but it was alright. It opened up my eyes. I had time to really put the pieces together and to organize my day and get into a routine.

Once you get into a routine and you got it going on, you know that this is the way you are going to discipline yourself. Rather than serving time, you get time to serve for you. But you see, you gotta go in there with something. I went in there with nothing but hope.

If you go in there with nothing, then you're going to be tossing and turning. You don't have much to go by but what the old cats are telling you. You have to have your values together. For me, jail was a great coolout. It gave me a chance to really review my life, and kinda set my sights on what I wanted to do.

Meanwhile the Poets were having their upheaval. There was a lot of divisive stuff going on. Kain, David, and Felipe felt slighted because they had been part of the first album, *The Last Poets,* and were now being excluded. Consequently, they—Kain, David, and Felipe, with the assistance of Woodie King—produced an album entitled *Right On! The Original Last Poets.*

I was getting information about those battles from my wife, and mother of my son Pharoah. She was writing me letters telling me about all these wild things that were happening. She also explained that Nilija, the conga player, was really the only one who was looking out for my interests, making sure I got the initial royalty check. I had to give permission to my lawyer to let my wife have the check.

I found that kind of peculiar because I thought it would be automatic that she would get it, but he said there are some cases where wives, when their husbands are in prison, take their money for their own uses. I could believe this since "other things" *were* done with my money.

But it was OK, it all turned out fine in the end, because everybody was healthy and strong, and kept their lives going on. My son is with me today. It was all good.

I didn't go through a torture chamber in jail or prison. I was there for three years and nine months. Dig it. I was only there three years and nine months with a 12–20 sentence, cause I was good. I was good in everything. I was a good person, I had a good spirit. I didn't talk to anybody—nobody even hardly heard my voice. I wasn't a "yes" person, cause that's not who I am, but I did mind my own business. I wrote every day. I was never late for count times; matter of fact when count time came, I was already up. I never got into a beef with anybody; if it looked like there could be a beef I quickly defused it somehow. There was no question. I worked in the prison hospital. Every test that I took I got an A+. It was like I was a very serious model prisoner. I was a model prisoner to the point where when I got out, they asked me to come back and speak to the prisoners.

I was in Central Prison, North Carolina, which is called "The Wall." 835 West Morgan Street, to be exact. And one of the brothers who helped me get out of prison is now the head sheriff of Raleigh, and that's John Baker. He was a bad brother. He played for the Pittsburgh Steelers. He was a big, bruisin, bad Black brother. He knew I shouldn't have been in prison. The guards knew, too. The racist, white, cracker Klan guards knew I shouldn't have been in prison.

They treated me different than the others. If I had mail, all I had to do was go look under my pillow. If there was no mail under my pillow,

I had no mail. Perry, the guard, would take it out of the bunch and he would put it under my pillow. I never talked to Perry beyond anything. If I said anything, I was cool, I was polite, I was cordial. I treated him like you treat someone that you meet in the elevator. It was never no passion, I didn't ask about his wife or kids or nothing. I knew he was a cracker from some swampy area in North Carolina. I was a Black guy, probably a "nigger" in his mind, from New York. But I was a cool nigger and he was a cool cracker. He was doing his job. He was in charge of that cell block. He had the gear and he acted like that was the only job he was ever born for. Didn't bother me. Didn't intimidate me. We never had a beef, and the best respect I could ever imagine came from this cracker, and I don't know many brothers who can claim that about a white man. I had pretty good instincts about people, even though I wasn't raised with my father.

My real father? I've never seen him. I'm not going to have no poor pity party over the fact that I never seen the guy. I don't know anything about him. At one time, I suppose, my father was a real mystery to me. However, since I prefer being clear-headed and responsible, it has really eliminated a lot of that stuff associated with an absent father. If you like yourself, then you don't have time to be crying about what didn't happen and what you don't have.

I think everything that happened to me was supposed to happen. I feel very blessed. People want to make a case—"Well, he did this because he never knew his father." I didn't see it like that. Whatever he was or wasn't is of no consequence to me. Maybe it was good that I've never seen him. I've gotten all the tools that I need to be who I am and feel good about me. I don't have no little animals coming to me or little demons in the middle of the night making me do strange stuff.

I did have a man in my life. I've had men in my life to give me guidance and to help me discover the man in me. That is all that's required of one. I mean, if it's not the biological cat that helped bring you into manhood, so what? I don't get bent out of shape and I don't see big soap operas for that. Everybody has the opportunity to have a man or woman in their lives, and they should seek these important relationships if it's a need.

That's what happened with me and Daddy Joe. As much as I talk bad about him, I could not have had a more impacting man in my life.

Actually, whenever I go through changes in my personal life, I have a particular part of a Psalm I always say:

Goodness and mercy shall follow me all the days of my life
And I should dwell in the house of the Lord forever.

Although I deeply believe in these words, sometimes I have to remind myself to say them regularly. I'm not coming from a religious place. I don't go to church on Sundays. I'm not down with all of the things that they say Jesus said. But there are certain things that are truths that touch me and that I can relate to. And this passage is one of them. My life has been just like that—goodness and mercy have followed me every day of my life, and I've been living in the house of the Lord ever since I've been here.

I look forward to continuing in the house of the Lord, even though sometimes it gets awfully dark and dreary and it gets kind of shaky and it gets very moody. I am blessed and I know that. I have always been blessed; I mean, I had two mothers—my aunt and my real mother.

Ain't no way in the world I could complain. I had a "mother" when I was a child, and when I got grown and my aunt died, "Mommy," my biological mother, took over. She is now the closest person in my life. If you look at her, you see me. Look at me, you see her. I mean it's obvious, we're mother and son. It's a beautiful thing. I'm so thankful the Gods have given me space and time to grow up with her. We're the two oldest in our family, here in New York. Everybody else has passed on or lives in Cincinnati.

Now, back to being a Last Poet. I feel that we deserve a lot because we've done a lot. But my feeling is I've never felt slighted, cheated, or short-changed, not one second, even though people expect me to feel that way. The work is bigger than I am. Being a Last Poet has been a blessing for me. I've been fortunate to be able to have an opportunity to express myself in words that came out of my experiences—out of my mouth, out of my mind—and for people to actually appreciate that stuff to the point where they want to hear it again.

I do not see myself as being somebody society owes. I think that it was my ignorance that caused me to be in difficulties, in terms of why I'm not receiving the monies for work done when I was a kid. I think that it was pure ignorance, and basically because I didn't choose to be astute in the business side of things.

I was truly in line with my reality back then, which was that there was going to be a revolution and that all of this stuff was going to be ashes and we were going to have a brand-new world. I was truly on a mission in terms of just dealing with what I felt I must be about, and monetary things didn't have very much to do with it. Now I'm grown. I've got children. I've got responsibilities, and I must try to fulfill them. These days there's this talk of getting what's due you because your album has been out for twenty-five years and you haven't gotten any royalties. People have sampled my work so others are asking if I feel bad that they're getting rich and I'm not. I don't feel bad, and I feel I'm going to get paid eventually.

I believe the work I'm doing today is good quality. If the Gods bless us like they have been, it seems then I'm going to get my just due, and I will be pleased.

I don't look forward to robbing the bank, per se, but I do look forward to living comfortably and passing something on to my children. I also want to do something good with some of the wealth that should come from my efforts. Above that, the work is still paramount. We are serious about this message and what our mission is: to try to change the way we think about ourselves as a race of people and the way other people think about us.

Umar Bin Hassan, 1993. (Courtesy of Thi-Linh Le)

UMAR BIN HASSAN
PERSONAL STATEMENT

I was born Jerome Huling on October 30, 1948, in Akron, Ohio, at Akron City Hospital. My father, Gilbert Roland Huling, was twenty when he and my seventeen-year-old mother, Barbara Jean Fuller, were starting out. Soon after I was born, I remember my father went away for a little while. He went to prison for armed robbery. Then we lived with my father's people, Elizabeth and Willie Huling. It was sometimes tragic.

My grandfather, who was very intelligent and thoughtful, loved to read. He knew the Bible back and forth. The preacher, Reverend Butler at the Furnace Street Mission, used to come and get ideas for his sermons from my grandfather. My grandmother could be one of the most insensitive, difficult, evil women you'd ever meet in your life. She seemed like she was set to destroy all the men in the Huling family. She had no respect for my grandfather; she humiliated him in public.

My father was a skillful musician who could read and write music, which was a novelty in the 1950s. When the Big Bands would come to town, they'd ask him to sit in. His thing was trying to get support and trying to get belief out of his mother. She always beat him down and told him, "You should get a job. Fuck music. You don't know nothing about music." That's what really destroyed my father—he never got her love or support. He was a hell of a musician, a hell of an artist, but no one gave him support. He was going through changes. He wanted his mother to believe in him and she wouldn't. He was artistic and very, very sensitive. He was in the wrong time, the wrong town, and the wrong family, so he didn't get what he needed, so he started taking his frustrations out on us, his own family.

After my grandmother had beat down him and my grandfather, she saw I had some initiative, so she came after me. One of my aunts told me, just three years ago, that my grandmother didn't like me, because she couldn't beat me down. "She didn't like you, you got away from her," my aunt said. When others in the family would extol my virtues as a child, my grandmother's thing was always to discourage me as much as possible. The best thing I ever heard her say about me was I'm not shit, and I'm never going to be shit.

I learned how to deal at two and three years old. That's what fucks me up now; when people abuse children and think they won't realize it or remember it. Children and animals can see when someone's out to hurt them. They can feel it instinctually.

I'd run and hide sometimes from my grandmother. I learned to protect myself at a young age. Fuck that, people are bullshitting anyway. They say they love you when they have contempt for you. I got most of my sharp tuning early on. I always knew, no matter how close people were to me, I could always tell when they were bullshitting me. I always got back at them, when they weren't expecting it. I learned to protect myself early.

I grew up in the Elizabeth Park projects, the "Bottom," in North Akron, Ohio. There were six apartments in my building; there were the Wilsons, the Andersons, the Arnolds, the Jeffersons, the Waters, and the Hulings. It seemed like almost every week, one family was fighting another family. It was the Waters against the Andersons or the Wilsons against the Arnolds, or the Jeffersons against the Hulings, or the Hulings against the Arnolds. That was just the way it went in North Akron, in the projects. It didn't matter if you were sensitive, nice, and kind, that was bullshit. You either learned to throw down or you got dogged. I was sensitive and I wanted to be nice. I didn't want to fight. I was scared to fight, then I got to a point when all I wanted to do was kick someone's ass.

But there were people in North Akron in the projects that took a liking to me. Two specific men come to mind. One was Richard Neal. He was a coach and gym instructor at the Elizabeth Park gymnasium. The other was Bill Suddeth; he was a park policemen. Sometimes they saw I was very raw and riled and cruel, but they—Mr. Neal especially—were the first to see the athletic ability in me. We had a little basketball team in the projects and we would go to the Y and play all the white boys from the Catholic teams. I was on the first team. I was really good at it. We were really good at it. We were the best team in the league.

But Mr. Neal also noticed I had a temper. He knew my family background and the pain I was living with and sometimes when I went off, he'd understand, but sometimes he'd say, "You know, Huling, you just always want to fight," or "Jerome, why do you always want to fight?" I got in a fight with anyone who would say anything to me or not say the right thing to me. I was ready to fight. Richard and Bill are the two men that tried to change me at a very early age. Somewhat surrogate fathers, they tried to look after me and guide me. They knew my father and knew what he was going through with his family so they kinda looked out for me.

I was learning shit from people in the streets. Whores and pimps were teaching me things. There were other games, too: white men would try to seduce and molest us kids, but we'd end up taking their money. They were the most degrading and depraved motherfuckers you ever saw. You just had to hit 'em in the head with the shoeshine box and they'd give us their money. Once we beat up a white man. We were beating him bloody, and when we figured he was ready to surrender and give us his money he said, "Don't stop, I like it." That was my first and last experience with sadomasochism.

I did shoe-shining when the family's welfare check ran out. Sometimes it was so cold—snow up to my knees, cold winds, and I didn't have no boots, or gloves. I had to go out and bring food back for seven brothers and sisters at eight years old, so I had to find other hustles. I learned how to help prostitutes with finding men. I did breaking and entering. These were things that helped bring in money. That was the most paramount thing to me: helping the Huling family survive. Sometimes I would bring home some salami and bread and juice. I fed my family. I gave my father money to buy cigarettes. Then I'd save little bit and he'd steal it. I took a lot on as a small child, until I left home at nineteen.

I began to resent my father. I would play with him in his moments of disillusionment. I was beginning to play mind games with people. There were times he'd grab me, start smacking me—smacking me in the face. At first I would cry, but the more he began to do it, the stronger I became. There was one time he just started smacking me and I had gotten so used to it, I just started laughing and he looked at me and said, "You know, you're a crazy little nigga."

When I was shining shoes, the other shoeshine boys would go home at 8 or 9 o'clock. I'd stay out till the bars closed. I wasn't going to let those hillbillies believe they were smarter than me. The hill-billies from West Virginia and Kentucky didn't like us. They could hardly speak good English, had no imagination, but they were like, "You niggas!" I didn't go by what they said when they'd yell, "Nigga, you can't come in." I was shining shoes, I needed that money. It wasn't personal; it was business. I always went in to those bars and shined those shoes. They never scared me. Those hillbillies would spit on me, kick me, and call me all kinds of names, but I still kept coming. One day, one of the owners of one of those bars asked me what my name was. I told him it was Jerome. He said, "No, you're not Jerome—from now on you're Geronimo. You're a Black Indian." That has given me strength to this day.

There were barmaids who were my surrogate mothers. There was one barmaid, her name was Eunice and she worked in the High Hat Bar. Her skin was so black. She was the prettiest Black woman I've ever seen, with the whitest teeth.

Eunice was in love with a light-skinned brother named John who played baseball in the park. They made a helluva couple. These sisters looked out for me. I would stay out til 3 in the morning. There was a little alleyway, Spring Street, that led to the projects. No one went through there, except me—singing. One night, my father was looking for me. I was halfway up Spring Street when I saw him coming, and I knew he was mad. When he was mad, he walked real fast. I was sitting under the bridge counting my money. When he got up on me, he said, "Boy, what are you doing? Come on home. Come with me." I thought, he's really gonna whip my ass. When we got home, he turned around, looked at me, then he looked at my mother and said, "This little nigga is crazy." I wasn't crazy, but I was growing up with the pain from my father and grandmother. That night my father could see I was getting strong.

Around age eleven, I started saying, "Wait a minute. I ain't mad at you for beating Mommy, but if you ain't gonna be the man, you gotta go. If I'm doing all this hustling and feeding this family, I'm gonna be the man here." I told my mother, "I'mma kill Daddy. He's gotta go, because he's not doing what he should as a man."

She thought I was playing. To prove her wrong I went to this place called Western Auto Store and I boosted—stole—a little boy scout hatchet with a nice little weight to it. I decided I was gonna kill my daddy with it. I took it home and showed it to my mother and she laughed and said, "You ain't gonna do nothing to your daddy."

The police were always giving my father restraining orders to stay away from my mother, but he was like, "This is my house, I'm a Black man," so, he'd still come in. On this night, he decided to come home and break the rules. I decided that was the night to kill him.

He broke the door and broke the window. I ran downstairs. There was a couch by the door; I jumped on the couch and just as he was coming in—and you know I'm a Scorpio, and when a Scorpio says they're gonna love you or kill you, they're gonna do that for real. I was very strong for my young age. My mother saw I was serious. She ran down and grabbed the hatchet from me and he thought *she* was gonna hurt him, so he chased her back upstairs and beat her up and then left, when it was really me who was gonna do it.

My mother took that beating. She told me she did so because I would have been real sorry for the rest of my life for killing him.

When I was about fourteen, we left the projects. My mother and father broke up. We moved in with my mother's mother, Rose Fuller. She was the first strong person—real strong person—in my life. She was the one who taught me about a sense of family. I loved my grandmother because she cared for us. She didn't have to take us in, but she did. If she hadn't taken us in, who knows what would have happened to us. Another life began for me at 339 West Chestnut on the west side of Akron, and I went to West Jr. High School, where I really began to get into athletics.

I was into football and track. I left West and went to South High School and I became a track and football star there. High school was probably the most turbulent time in my life. I was going through a lot of changes. What was I gonna do? Was I gonna leave Akron? Was I gonna stay in Akron and get a job in the rubber factories? The only thing that kept me in school was athletics. I really didn't get into the academic side. I found high school uneventful. It was boring. Everything I was learning was about someone else. All the teachers, principals, and counselors knew Jerome "Hank" Huling had intelligence. It just seemed like all I wanted to be was a nigger.

I got away with a lot as an athlete. I told everybody it was all just play football, run track, and get pussy—and that's all I did. Even though I gave it a halfhearted and half-assed effort in high school and on the football field, there were still people interested in me. They wanted me to go to their colleges, because they could see the potential, but I wasn't ready to get recruited. I knew sports was just a business after high school. I saw brothers who went to college and hurt their leg, became a physical liability, and were thrown back into the street.

When I was seventeen years old, no one in the world liked being a nigger more than Umar. I was totally into drama, and South High School was my stage. Probably one of my most dramatic moments was when I became Homecoming King. I was kickin' it with Inez Paul at the time. Inez Paul was the total opposite of who I was. She was sweet, well-mannered, and liked by everyone. Inez liked me, so when she was chosen to be the Homecoming Queen, she made it known that Hank Huling was to be her escort. Hank was to be King.

The principal in the high school was an Italian guy—Sicilian. He wanted to be white so bad, but he looked like a nigga. He had nappy hair and thick lips. He'd say, "I'm Italian, I'm Italian." I would go up to him and say, "Do you know who your people are in Sicily?" That would burn this man up. He'd turn red, black, blue, everything. He didn't like me, so when the Homecoming Queen said she wanted me to be Homecoming King, he said, "No, no!"

My boys found out and staged a demonstration. I love those niggas still for this. They were my partners: Reggie Watson, Matthew Pugh (Uncle Bud), Willie Johnson, Eugene Mitchell, Andre Reed, and Marvin Minner. They all made signs reading "We Want Hank," "Hank Is King," and they picketed the principal's office and won. I was Homecoming King. It left a bad taste in most of the student body's mouth. That was the best thing that ever happened to me in high school.

All I remember about my school years was I danced a lot, told jokes, and got through—barely. I graduated with three C's, a D, and an F. They passed me because they wanted me out of that school. I would do things that nobody else would do, just to prove a point. Even my friends sometimes got worried about me. They'd say, "Hank, why you do the shit you do?" I would do shit just because. Why be afraid?

No one can stop you from being who you are. I remember one day during lunch period we were all standing around laughing and just kicking it. Then the Akron Police pulled up in a paddy wagon across the street. Everybody got scared. All the brothers got quiet. I looked and said, "Because these white boys pulled up in a paddy wagon, you're gonna stop being who you are?" I went across the street to their paddy wagon screaming, "I'm Stokely Carmichael's cousin! Black power! Black power!" I scared those white boys.

They didn't like that. They arrested me. I had to let those white boys know there's one in this crowd you can't intimidate and who's not afraid of you, who's gonna be who he truly is.

It just so happened that that was my lucky day. When they took me to the court, Richard Neal happened to be at court. They all respected him down there and he said, "I know this young boy." Because, see, white people have this thing, they want to know who knows this little nigga, does anybody know this little nigga? Mr. Neal, the "nice Negro"

22

at court said he knew me. He spoke up for me, and they let me go back to school. When I got back to school, I was a hero. I was Hank "Black Power!" Huling for the day.

Being out front has always been Umar Bin Hassan's thing. Sometimes I pay the price for it. I've lost families and sistas. Sistas in my life used to say, Umar, we want you to be like this—go to college. But, this is not me, sistas. I got to be who I am.

I fought against everybody. Now, I don't fight *everybody*. I realize there are people who care for me and want me to do the best I can do. I've paid the price of being called "crazy" and "uncontrollable." It's cool. If you're a true artist, you sacrifice yourself for mankind. Sometimes you do this to show them how to be human, but they think it's funny. However, you're showing them something important.

I used to really be insane; I have control now. I liked myself then, even though I was being inconsiderate and indifferent to everybody and tried to push people away. There were people who loved me. They are the mothers of my children. Queenie Mae, Janice, Malika, and Oni. There's so much I can say about these women. These were sistas who were with me in my most trying times, when I was really learning about myself as a person. As a human being I took them through changes. I was nice sometimes; I wasn't nice sometimes. I tried to understand sometimes; I didn't understand sometimes. But I tried to love them as much as possible.

The fact is that they honored me by giving me children and they've helped develop them into some of the best human beings and most intelligent young people on this planet. I can say that if it wasn't for these sistas when I was off into my own little world, my children wouldn't be the responsible, intelligent human beings they are. If there's one thing in this world that scares me—and there's not too much—is if these sistas ever got together and wrote a book about me. I'd be in trouble for real.

As a Black man in America, I've had to have intelligence, imagination, and sensitivity. This society doesn't want you to be sensitive—and especially a sensitive Black man. They want you to be an animal, growling and snarling. It's easier to deal with us that way. A Black man with sensitivity, imagination, and creativity is just a bit much. White people don't want it—even some brothers don't want it. And sometimes Black women, who say they want it, can't seem to believe it when you share it with them. You *can't* be sensitive, you're not supposed to be. This realization made me come to empathize with my father, and eventually I came to love him again despite the things he did to my mother and me.

For Senior Day, I wrote a poem about all my teachers and it blew everybody's mind. This is when I was getting into poetry. It was so unique and special that one teacher said, "See, Huling, if you could have used that talent in school, you could have been the smartest student in this school." I already knew that.

I was always a reader. I read things. I went to the library. My mother taught me to read, and she taught me how to use words. I used these skills when racist people in high school tried to offend me. I upset them. They thought I didn't know nothing. I was no one's dumb nigga.

I got a job at Firestone Tire and Rubber after I graduated from high school. I went to Akron University, part-time, because my mother wanted me to. I hated college. I hated the niggers, white and black, sitting there playing spades; talking about how many hours they were taking; and what they were gonna be. Man, I thought, do you niggers really know what's up? They thought they were gonna get *in* because they were educated. I hated that, so I quit Akron University.

I had always been interested in the workings of the mind and how far you could stretch it and test it. I remember there was a professor who used to come on TV. He was a heavy white boy. He really got to me. I connected with him. One day, I'm going across the campus and I'm looking and I see a cap flying in the wind. I get closer and it's him—the professor. He has a hat on his head like a pirate and I see he has some Puss 'N Boots costume on. Seeing him in that getup, I thought, let me get the fuck out of here.

I had a job. I had a car, music, my J&B, reefer, and Black beauties. I would go to Cleveland and just hang out. I couldn't hang in Akron; it was too slow for me. The Cleveland Black people were just my speed. Don King is from there. Cleveland got me ready for the big city. Cleveland Black people loved to rap. Plus they had girls who didn't play no games. If they liked you, they gave it up. There was the Red Circle ballroom on Euclid Avenue. I remember a guy pulled a sawed-off shotgun on me for feeling his woman's butt—he was mad because she liked it. I liked to talk, so I talked my way out of it. When he walked away, I shot at him. He was a silly nigga to let me go.

Cleveland was the place where I began to get in contact with the Nationalist thing. Ahmed Evans was a leader of the Hough riots in Cleveland, just one of the many racially incited riots that were breaking out in cities across America. He told me about being Black and how to become more Nationalist. I didn't want to hear that. Fuck niggers, I don't care about that, I thought. He made me see that there's much more to it than that. I was hating my job. I had a hillbilly supervisor and a bunch of Black people who loved the job; I hated that. The more I hung with Ahmed Evans, the more I became politically conscious. I eventually became a militant. I hooked up with some other brothers in Akron and we started the Black United Front in Akron. We stirred some things up; we made people realize what was happening politically.

I had gotten into my Black militancy and was tired of hustling the streets. I was most influenced by Amiri Baraka. I saw him during the Newark riots. There was a picture of him in *Newsweek* magazine. His head was bandaged and he was bleeding and under the picture it read, "Smash those jelly white faces." The picture and the caption made me begin to write and think about being a little more conscious.

The first time I saw The Last Poets was in Yellow Springs, Ohio. They were what I needed. I was in the right place at the right time. I met Abiodun and Gylan Kain in 1968 at Antioch College at the Black Arts Festival. I was head of security there. That particular day, I felt the aggression of the street. I was packed: I had a .38 and a .45. Dun came up to the door and said, "I'm a Last Poet from New York City." I replied, "I don't care who you are, I'm head of security. Listen brother, you gonna get checked or you're gonna check out." Later when Dun was on stage, he dissed me: "Who's that crazy muthafucka at security?" I thought, homeboys' got some flava. Their poetry made me understand what people mean now when they say The Last Poets affect them. At that moment, I knew I wanted to be a Last Poet.

Gylan Kain, Felipe Luciano, Abiodun Oyewole, and Nilija helped me to make a decision on what I wanted to do, and where I wanted to be. I wanted to be a Last Poet, and I wanted to be a Last Poet in Harlem. However, first I had to go through something in my hometown, something that would supply me with the passion and the willpower to do just that.

At the time, Fred Ahmed Evans was my mentor. He always told us that when the shit broke out in Cleveland, he was going to be on the rooftops trying to shoot as many white police as possible, which is exactly what he did during the Hough Riots. Ahmed died in the penitentiary. I will always admire him, because he was one of the few who kept their word.

The Hough riots were some of the worst riots in this country. The same thing that was going on in Cleveland was going on in Akron. Police oppression, police brutality, and police indifference to the rights of Akron's Black citizens. This is why we formed the Black United Front. We had our headquarters on Wooster Avenue, the same avenue that some of us used to hustle and style on. We made a change. We didn't want to be niggers anymore. We wanted to be Black Men. So, when the shit hit the fan in Cleveland, it made its way down to Akron.

Rumor was, the police had beat up a couple of young brothers after a party. In those days, all it took was a rumor and the shit was on. We battled the police. Matter of fact, we put up such a battle they had to call in the National Guard. We battled them, too. We battled them in the projects. We battled them on Wooster Avenue, in Perkins Woods Park, on Raymond Street, on Bell Street, on Douglas Street, and up and down Euclid Avenue. Shots were fired. Some of us had hardware—they weren't equal to what the National Guard had—but we had heart, and we had a cause.

This went on for three or four days. Steadily the police and the National Guard gained the upper hand. They had more manpower and better strategy. We played the nuisance factor and we played it quite well—for beginners. A part of our strategy was holding up in our headquarters after curfew. The police didn't like that. But technically, we were off the streets. Still, the police didn't like that. They wanted us out of the building and off the avenue when the curfew came on. They found a way to accomplish it. As usual, they found one of us who didn't like being one of us, who was one of the so-called first Black policemen on the Akron police force.

This Negro policeman came up to our door and began his negotiations, but before he could finish, these hillbillies pushed him out of the way. They came in on us with gas, gas masks, billy clubs, and rifle butts. It was hand-to-hand for a while. I am still very proud of these brothers and sisters who fought. We were beaten back, but we were not beaten down. The police piled us into the paddy wagon. There was not enough room for all of us, but they didn't care. They started dropping gas in through the vents while everybody was trying to be as strong as possible. There were too many bodies and not enough air. Some of us passed out; the rest of us tried to keep the others from doing the same. It was a ride to jail I will never forget.

When I got to the holding cell, I saw people bloodied and bruised and burned by gas, clothes torn off, and smiles on their faces. There were smiles all around. Everyone was just elated that we had stood up to the police. They could never take us for granted again. Most of us got out on bail, except those of us who had bench warrants.

Afterwards, talks began with the city fathers and certain Negro leaders to discuss police brutality and other injustices. As usual, we were sold out by our more "responsible" Negro brothers. In the end we got two basketball courts and a night concert on Wooster Avenue. So much for the revolution in Akron.

I lost my job at Firestone Tire and Rubber Company because of my "criminal activities." I was depressed for days. No more job in a dirty, stinking rubber factory. Boo hoo. I knew it was time for me to leave. But what really helped me make up my mind was the recruitment letter I got from none other than the Akron Police Department.

My mother read the letter. I read the letter. We both just looked at each other. Time to go, baby boy. My mother knew. God bless her soul. That was the name of the game in my very right wing, Bible Belt, hillbilly, cracker hometown: If you can't shut 'em up, set 'em up. Goodbye, Akron. Hello, Last Poets and Harlem.

In February of 1969, when I first arrived in New York City on Forty-second Street, I saw all the lights and thought I was on Broadway. I asked someone was this Broadway, and he said something very important to me, probably the most important thing that has ever been said to me since I've been in New York these twenty-seven years: "This is Forty-Deuce Street, you better take your heart out and put it in your pocket." I had been hustling my whole life; if I could hustle on Forty-second Street, I could make it anywhere in New York City.

My first experience on Forty-second Street was when a Jamaican tried to play the money-in-handkerchief game with me. He must have thought, I got a real country nigga here. But us midwestern boys perfected all that out there. He gave me the money and I was gone. You give me a split second and an advantage, and I'm outta there. I took off running up 8th Avenue to 43rd and then to 9th Avenue. I hid in the park. After five minutes the Jamaican came looking for me with the police. I had beat him—there was $100 in the handkerchief.

I took the #2 train up to Harlem. I got out on 125th and Lenox Avenue. I went to The Last Poets' loft, the East Wind. I remember there was a Peoples drugstore on the corner. Even though it was winter, there were a lot of Black people out with so many styles, moving in so many directions. It knocked me up against the wall. Harlem was my playground. All this land!

I made my way to The Last Poets' loft. I found out that Gylan Kain, David Nelson, and Felipe had left. There was just Dun and Nilija; they remembered me from the college incident. I said I had no place to go, so Dun gave me $20 and said I could go with him.

That made me believe in him. He took me with him and his woman. A lot of brothers would have given you $20 and told you go ahead and do what you've got to do. He took me to a place on Riverside Drive. The next day he got me hooked up in a dorm for people in need of a place to stay until they found a home. It was the Alamac Hotel on 71st and Broadway.

One night when I was at the dorm, Dun and Nilija came down. They were getting ready to do a show that night, at which Dun told the audience, "There's a brother here from Ohio. You decide if he's a Last Poet." I had two poems. One was called "Nigger Town," and the other was called "Muthafucka."

I performed "Muthafucka." It was very crude and very strong. It had an adjective for every leader. It went:

Huey was a bad Muthafucka.
Malcolm was a royal Muthafucka. etc. . . .

It got over. People could see it was kinda crude, but they could see my sensitivity and my sincerity, commitment and dedication, so they responded, "Yeah, make him a Last Poet." That's how I became a Last Poet. So me and Dun started working together and then three or four months later, I met Jalal and he had some poetry and said he wanted to join us, so we listened. At first I didn't like Jalal. I thought he was corny.

But Dun had this thing about always operating in a trinity of poets, so we brought him in. It was him, myself, Dun, and the conga player, Nilija, who recorded the album *Last Poets* in 1970.

I began to hook up with a lot of sisters. One sister, Cookie, got me a job working with her at Harlem Teams for Self-Help. Cookie was sweet. She cared for me. Only thing that fucked it up was I was out trying to get in everybody's drawers. Harlem was such a cornucopia of people. Cookie and I were together for a year, then she moved on. Cookie realized I was a celebrity and getting silly. I was silly, but I was having fun. I was onstage and I was the Prince of Harlem. The Last Poets were the Princes of Harlem. People wanted to take us out, give us dinner. They knew what we were saying was coming from them, and they took us into their hearts.

Friction between Dun and Jalal developed. Jalal wanted to be like Miles, as he put it, and that pissed off Dun, who then decided to go off and do his political thing. It was me and Jalal and Nilija left in the group, and we did another album in 1971, entitled *This Is Madness.* Then, me and Jalal went through things. I left. Not only were they doing things, I was doing things that I didn't like, such as taking in all these sisters, smoking all the reefer, all the while telling everybody else how to get themselves together.

I was tired of this and began to reprimand them about things we were doing, and they didn't like it. They felt that I wasn't old enough to understand all the things they were doing and what it was all about. They thought I was just going through some changes, but I was very serious. I thought that we should live up to our word and live up to our credo as Last Poets. I thought we should try to do the right thing, you know, for our people and our communities.

We almost came to blows one day in a hotel in DC. I felt we should not be doing some of the things that we were doing. I left the group again, and then I came back. Suliaman was in the group when I returned. He didn't want me to come back. However, I made another album with them in 1974, entitled *At Last*. I left again in 1974. I was working with other groups and doing my own thing. I went through three marriages and had five children.

I was into the Islamic thing for a while. It touched me, like it touches a lot of brothers who come out of the streets. The religion touches you because the first thing you learn is how to let go of arrogance, indifference, harshness, and coldness. For those who can grasp the whole idea, it lets you give yourself to your lord and to find your true power. After a time, I became disillusioned with the movement, and next thing I knew I was back in the streets.

Sometime later I became depressed. I felt a lot of brothers were bullshitting and playing games where the revolution was concerned. I came from, Akron, Ohio, to be down with real brothers, but everyone was playing games—the Muslims, the Nationalists. I was also involved with a woman at the time, and we weren't getting along, either. The disillusionment sent me back to the streets.

First, I started selling cocaine, then taking it, then addicted to it, then smoking it. Then I got to a point where I was sitting in crack houses looking at everyone else, thinking they're taking this shit personally. They're not coming back from this.

These were times when I didn't want to be a Last Poet, but I couldn't get away from it. I used to give poetry readings in crack houses. People would say, "Ain't you . . . ?" I would encourage them to get to the first blast to avoid the question.

This was just a test as far as I was concerned, but some people were really getting into it, believing this is how we're supposed to be. We're supposed to be crack addicts, because we didn't get degrees from high school and we didn't get jobs. We're supposed to act like this. I felt I wasn't like this. I had to get up out of this little by little. I didn't want to get stuck out there. I've seen people degenerate from snorting cocaine to smoking cocaine to raping sisters and molesting young Black children. I didn't want to go no further. I didn't want to hurt sisters or children.

This all happened over a period of eight years and throughout seven states—New York, Connecticut, Pennsylvania, Massachusetts, Washington, DC, Michigan, Virginia. At one point, I almost accepted it. I'd snort it and, when I couldn't snort enough, I was smoking it. I was all messed up.

I went from freebasing cocaine and drinking cognac to crack and Old English, real quick. But then I made up my mind to get up out of there, day by day, by beginning to believe in myself again. Sometimes people don't want you to get well, so they can have someone to point to. It was OK to have Umar as the village idiot.

During my cracked-out days, the Poets had heard rumors that I had been shot to death; that I was gay; that I was the police. In 1990, Dun, Felipe, and Kain were together when I came back to New York to find Jalal had stolen my publishing rights from me. Dun had taken one of my poems, "Time," and had given it to a rap group, A Tribe Called Quest, to sample. Gregory Reed, a lawyer in Detroit had granted permission. Dun felt it was in part his poem, since they thought I was dead. Jalal had stolen all of Dun's poetry, too. He said he had the rights. When I first came back, these were all people I wanted to kill.

Producer Bill Laswell was introduced to me through Jalal and Suliaman (who appeared together in the film *Poetic Justice*). I met Bill and he was skeptical. He knew I was on drugs, but he saw me trying. We got together. That solo album, *Be Bop or Be Dead*, opened the door for The Last Poets to come back. I began to talk to Bill. He's very creative and productive and his thing was he had been trying for twenty years to get us back together. He was using money out of his pocket. He said he wanted to lay down some stuff.

He felt my voice was still there and asked me to do a solo album. When Jalal and Suliaman found out, they got upset. I didn't give a fuck. It was my turn now. Later on, Dun and I got together and recorded "Holy Terror" at Bill's suggestion.

The work is now out there. Me and Dun have been doing all the hard work and not getting paid and doing Lollapalooza and trying to bring The Last Poets back together, because we love doing this. Because we love sharing ourselves with people. We may offend somebody or say something that sounds homophobic or anti-Semitic, but actually we care for everybody in our audience. We're poets. We're artists.

The Poetry of The Last Poets

THE DRUM PRAYER

When the heart beats
the river flows
raised by fire
heat is heard . . .

—Don "Babatunde" Eaton

TO OUR PEOPLE

We are the rhythm, we are the words, we are the
language. We're the flavor, we are the spices, we
represent all of the attitudes and all of the generating
life force. We give vibration to this land.

A.M.

*This is probably the most pivotal poem of my career. I had just gotten
back to New York in the winter of 1990 after some time "in the
streets." People had stolen from me, probably hoping that I wasn't
alive so they could get away with something. These were my so-called
brothers who were supposed to know better. One had sold all my pub-
lishing, saying it was he who had written all my poetry on the first and
second albums. Another "brother" had a bullshit lawyer friend from
Detroit, who sold part of my poem "Time" for sampling to the rap
group A Tribe Called Quest. He said he heard I was dead. Did I get
mad? No. I got high. I had just come back from the World of Drugs
and Violence. I didn't need to be putting my hands on anybody. I
couldn't afford to be negative. I had so many positive things I wanted*

to do. So, I went out and began to get high again. Drugs became my friend. Drugs have always been my friend, when I believed in no one else. When I trusted no one else, I trusted drugs. Addiction in America is an elite club. Forever let us wave our banners: high, high, high. During that period, I was in between. One night I'd do a show. The next night I'd be at the crack house. But I didn't hurt, harm, or steal from anyone. I kept all the pain to myself. In spite of all this, I was determined to do what I came to New York to do: put The Last Poets back on the right track and record a solo album.

—UBH

A.M.

The media has been alerted to the brave new World
with action-packed comedies full of Navy Seals and Dirty Blondes.
Welcome to the Revolution where ex-CIA madmen go AWOL in
children's cartoons.
No deposit! No return!
A sickness prevails in the land.
The keepers of the watch are fondling the children.
Youthful madness chasing games around the fire.
40-ounce grins dripping with the sacrifice of innocence.
The blood in their eyes smile so defiantly at their wounds. Teasing and
following laughter to its death. Dancing in the joys of casual violence
and the polite discussions of their senseless acts. Screaming songs of
Champagne and bigtime into the dreams of open sores that lurk and
scheme in the shadows of clouds of smoke. Begging for slow rides in
silent ambulances to well-stocked morgues where rhythm and
blues . . . oozes out of muted loud-speakers.

Wholesale genocide at discount prices.
America
love it or leave it.
Bloated egos with small minds baptizing murder in the name of God
and everything we hold sacred. Mickey Mouse! Donald Duck!
Forever let us wave our banners high . . . high . . . high!
Sitting here in the midst of falling leaves, overwhelmed by this
symphony of freedom.
Letting go . . . Letting go . . . of others who want to claim all of this
as their own. A rat makes its presence known keeping all things real.

Screeching and scurrying to nowhere fast. Trapped in its own greed and grandiose visions of self-destruction.
Women caressing jagged tears while kissing their frustrations with stolen moments. Their pain . . . exploding into the darkness of shall I try this one more time?

Cocaine has become the Law and Order of Big Business and corruption riding through the streets on the frowns of rookie cops who relieve their frustration in the cold-blooded antics of shoot-to-kill! My country . . . 'tis of thee . . .

Sweet land of Napalm and unwritten poems of Soprano saxophones crying for those whose tears are stuck in reverse and the latest cable TV channel. And I hear the voice of nature whisper, the victory is yours if you want it.
The victory is yours if you want it.

Love the children in the beginning to save them in the end. Somewhere I hear a revival. Somewhere I hear bop playing. The voice across the waters. Standing in the dark. Minton was a shrine to the diaspora. Monk speaking in the tongues of his ancestors.

Denouncing the frail mediocrity of "you people" didn't come from anything. Somewhere I hear a revival. Somewhere I hear bop playing. It is playing in the hip-hop walks of young boys who hit strange notes with hands on triggers. BAM! . . . BAM! . . . BAM! . . .

Max picks up the beat. Rhythms from the bush. Passionate and vital information. Intense stares into the memories of Warriors . . . Lovers of children . . . and the protectors of the women who now seek protection in the distant and foreign fears of dying at the hands of desperate choices and stray bullets.

Bird lives . . . Bird lives . . . Bird lives . . . in the death to all you hip ofay lies lost in the darkness of oversized berets. Sucking my blood with your well-publicized and juvenile poetry. I play for the Gods . . . I play for Allah. I play for all those souls lost in your pretentious smiles and cool jazz as I continue my journey home. You stole my father. You stole my mother.

And now you try to deny this one last tribute to God. You will not rejoice in my death. You can't kill bop . . . the brotherhood is strong. Get 'em Junior. Get 'em Junior. Up jumps Miles bobbing and weaving. Sticking and moving. Going against traffic on a one-way street.

Loving . . . all the women in the crowd and in their dreams. Miles . . . the warm afterglow of an African Sunset. Someday my Prince will come. Someday my Prince will come. Miles turning his back on guaranteed death and low-life insinuations perpetuated by the perverted fantasies of the founding fathers of these United States of . . . Fuck you mothafuckas!
Fuck
you
mothafuckas! . . .
Miles was our gators and lizards. He was our silk shirts and Hickey Freemans. He was our cool slow walks into the wind. He was our

delicious smile on the face of extreme and bitter rejection. Get 'em Junior. Get 'em Junior.

That sound . . . What is that sound? So clean. So fluid. Emotions so hot in the passing of Summer into Autumn. The magnificence of awakening to something so rare . . . so new. Images dreaming softly in slow dances that wrap themselves so tightly around our doubts.
I touch your face.
You touch mine. He is so tender with our needs.
So strong in our desire to be free. The definitions of his statement colors the skyline. He was
that one last feeling of logic before needle punctured the vein. He was the music the morning after the resurrection of pain and prayers in the twisted honor and slight applause of demons and folk heroes stabbing us in the back.
He was a love Supreme.
He was a love Supreme.

And I hear the voice of Nature whisper, the victory is yours if you want it. The victory is yours if you want it. Somewhere I hear a revival. Somewhere I hear bop playing . . . in the faces of Southern old men full of Northern pain. It is Dizzy, Sonny, Jackie, Philly Joe, Kenny, Charlie, Clifford and many many more if you listen to the laughter of the children in the Projects and their sense of rhythm to survive. Bop is learning how to be yourself to feel the beauty inside. No more slick street games in the anticipation of growing . . . and pushing . . .
pushing . . . forward
coming into full expression.

.

Long way from home. So close to love. The spirit wants to move. My
mind frozen in worthless flesh. Back from the dead by Allah's mercy.
Leaving the Devil standing in the pain, leaving the pain alone. I give
my salaams to the right and left. Good has become a kind and loving
companion. Bad was only a test of faith. I now find strength in the
humility of this moment. This eternal moment of peace to all . . .
of those who come to understand that bop is love . . . and love . . . is
all . . . you are and ever will be. And I hear the voice of nature whisper,
the victory is yours
if you want it.
The victory is yours if you want it!

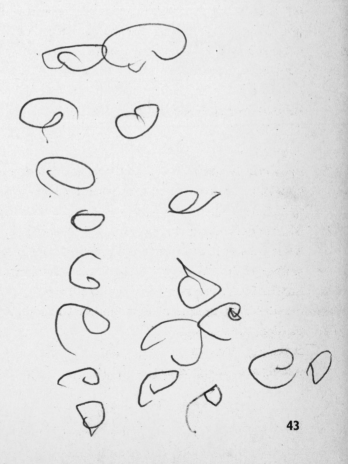

WHEN THE REVOLUTION COMES

We were getting ready for a revolution. There wasn't any question about whether there was going to be one or not. These were the heated sixties; tensions were thick. Just about everyone in the movement had a gun and knew how to make a Molotov cocktail (fire bomb). One of the comments of the day was: "Brother, do you have a match?" If the response was no, the crack was: "How you gonna start a revolution and you ain't even got a book of matches?" The revolution was inevitable.

Since Harlem was the Mecca of African American political and cultural events, many of us assumed the revolution would start there and spread like wildfire. Of course, being one of The Last Poets made me feel like I was at the vanguard of making this revolution happen. At the time, I was twenty years young, living on Hillside Avenue, in Jamaica, Queens. I used to drive my 1965 beige Impala through Grand Central Parkway across the Triboro Bridge to Harlem's 125th Street, each day. This in itself was a revolution to me. In my search for Black Power and Black dialogue I had heard a lot of people shout, rant, and rave about the need for revolution. "Fight fire, with fire!" they told us, but I hadn't fully understood the responsibilities of a revolution.

It was obvious to me that a drastic change had to take place if the majority of Blacks were going to experience real freedom. Many of us were familiar with the "systems" that were not going to benefit our people. We also knew that when a young America was fed up with England's teatime and taxes, they did something drastic about it.

The truth was, many of us still saw ourselves as "niggers" and slaves. This was a mind-set that had to change if there was ever to be Black Power. The major problem in the Black community was lack of unity. The fact is, we probably had just as many Black people working diligently for the system, as those fighting tooth and nail against it.

So there I was, on the front lines of this great would-be revolution. I thought, how could I be a catalyst for this Armageddon? I wondered, how can I say something that hasn't been said before? One of the most common expressions was, "When the Revolution comes." You'd hear it when you saw a brother with a big afro, dashiki, beads, and a white girl on his arm. Somebody would yell out: "You gonna have to get rid of Miss Ann, when the revolution comes, brother." Folks would break out in laughter. These moments inspired "When the Revolution Comes."

—AO

WHEN THE REVOLUTION COMES

When the revolution comes
some of us will catch it on TV
with chicken hanging from our mouths
you'll know it's revolution
because there won't be no commercials
when the revolution comes
preacher pimps are gonna split the scene
with the common wine stuck in their back pockets
faggots won't be so funny then
and all the junkies will quit their nodding
and wake up
when the revolution comes
transit cops will be crushed
by the trains after losing their guns
blood will run through the streets of Harlem
drowning anything without substance
when the revolution comes
Revolution is silent
I hope pearly white teeth fall out of the mouths
that speak of revolution without reference
the course of revolution is 360
understand the cycle that never ends
understand the beginning to be the end
and nothing in between but space and time
that I make or you make to relate or not to relate
to this world outside my mind, your mind
speak not of revolution until

you are willing to eat rats to survive
when the revolution comes
when the revolution comes
Black cultural centers will be forts
supplying the revolutionaries with food and arms
white death will fall off the walls
of museums and churches
breaking the lie that enslaved our mothers
when the revolution comes
jesus christ is gonna be standing
on the corner of Malcolm X Blvd. and 125 St.
trying to catch the first gypsy cab out of Harlem
when the revolution comes
afros will be straightening their heads
and straightened heads are gonna be trying to get afros
when the revolution comes
women are gonna look like women
and men are gonna look like men again
when the revolution comes
but until then you know and I know niggers will party and bullshit
and party and bullshit and party and bullshit and party
and some might even die
before the revolution comes.

RUN NIGGER

This was my first "Nigger" poem. I had started writing poetry in the sixth grade when my teacher Mr. Havilik mysteriously asked me to write a poem about graduation.

My early experience with poetry happened in high school when I felt a violent urgency to get older. Of course, this meant girls my age were too young to date, so I developed this attraction for older girls. I would try to impress them with my premature maturity as well as my poetic verse. It was during this time that the Civil Rights movement dominated the media. Martin had been awarded the Nobel Peace Prize and Black people were struggling. I was writing love poetry, but the social issues were starting to influence my pen.

"Nigger" was a key word. Nigger was the embodiment of all the anger, frustration, joy, and pain of being Black in America. It was more *than a word, it was a term with dimensions far beyond the negative connotations found in the dictionary. With all the color, attitude, excitement, strength, and shame, we knew we could not build a movement on Niggers or Niggerisms, although the concept of Nigger was constantly being redefined.*

Gylan Kain had given me my first decisive definition of Niggers as they relate to our liberation. His poem "Niggers Are Untogether People" is a known classic and will always be one of my favorite poems dealing with Niggers. David Nelson also documented the futility of Niggers and wrote a classic poem entitled "Die Nigga Die." Both of these poems were an inspiration for me. They introduced me to a language that I had not given serious attention to previously. With this aid, it was my turn to unveil my Nigger poem. How could I get started, I thought, what do Niggers do? And "Run Nigger" was born.

—AO

I understand that time is running out
I understand that time is running out
time is running out as hastily
as niggers run from the man
time is running out
on lifeless serpents
reigning over a living kingdom
time is running out of talks
marches tunes chants and prayers
time is running out of time
I heard someone say
things were changing
from Brown to Black
time is running out on Bullshit changes
running out like a brush fire in a dry forest
like a murderer from the scene of the crime
like a little roach from DDT
Time is running out
like big niggers run on a football field
Run Nigger
killing your children
Run Nigger
taking your life
Run Nigger
Run like you run
when the liquor store is closing
and it's Saturday night
Run Nigger

Run like time
never yielding or forgiving
moving forward
in progressive movements
never warning or relinquishing
Time is running running running
time's done run OUT!

IF WE ONLY KNEW

"Knowledge Is Power" the sign read. I had heard that expression hundreds of times, but this time it hit me in a different way. I guess you can say I thought about it a little deeper. What kind of knowledge is power? Knowledge of self? Knowledge of history? It dawned on me: Knowledge of truth is power.

There's an African parable that inspired this poem. The parable describes an eagle who had been raised with chickens and thereby grew up believing he was a chicken. He, of course, was larger than the other birds. His wingspan was much greater and his beak was much bigger. However, he still thought he was a chicken. He didn't even try to fly. He just walked around the chicken yard all day like the other chickens. One day an eagle from the mountains descended into the chicken yard and told the ignorant eagle that he was not a chicken and that he should flap his wings and fly away. He told him he could join his family up in the mountains. At first, the little eagle was afraid, but then he finally flew.

Metaphorically, I couldn't imagine a better story to describe Blacks who have bought the lie and see themselves only as they are told to. So "If We Only Knew" was aimed to empower those who have thought themselves powerless.

—AO

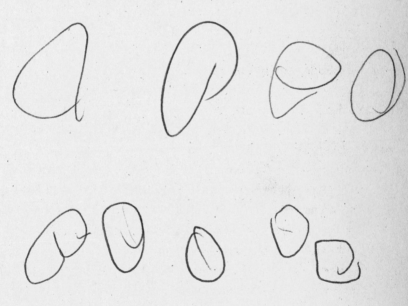

IF WE ONLY KNEW

If we only knew what we could do
We'd stop fussin and fightin and feelin blue
If we only knew that we have juice
Cause of an African connection
That we can't cut loose
If the light was on in our minds
We wouldn't dis ourselves so much all the time
We'd stop and realize without disguise
We got the power to change what's before our eyes
Where there is poverty and misery
We'd bring hope, joy, love and security
There wouldn't be no need to lock your doors at night
No one lives in the dark
Cause everyone sees the light
If we only knew just how bad we are
We'd make the sun disappear
Cause we're the brightest star
If we could feel the strength
And help those who are weak
And be steppin to the rhythm like Malcolm speaks
So you thought you were a chicken
And your butt was made for kickin
You been running around
With your head hanging down
Looking for chicken feed
In this city of greed
Open up your eyes
Don't you know you can fly

Like an eagle to the sky much higher than high
Where you don't need no crack, smack, or patty wack
And all the bones from that dog
You can give them right back
If we only knew what we could do

We'd stop fussin and fightin and feelin blue
Just like we cut our hair in an African style
We show rich, royal treasure every time we smile
Now sometime ago we just didn't know
That we had the power to make the whole thing go
Motivator, educator we're a power generator
We need to own the joint
Instead of working as a waiter
If we only knew how strong our will
No matter what's been done
Our souls can't be killed
Like the sun and the moon and all the stars above
It's a natural thing for us to share our love
We're a healing force in a world of pain
Trying to use common sense where like is insane
If we could recognize just who we be
We'd take control of our lives and live with dignity.

MY PEOPLE

I was coming of age, revolutionary age, that is. It seemed that ever since I had been in the Poets, I had been writing negative poetry. Poetry that dissected the problem, described it, and admonished those who were caught up in it. I had written "Run Nigger," "Gash Man," "New York New York," "Two Little Boys," "When the Revolution Comes," and a host of other poems revealing the lies, the sores, the problems. I remember being at a workshop at the East Wind when a brother said, "You can't be a real revolutionary unless you have an idea of the kind of world you want to build for your people. It's easy to tear down, but it's another thing to build up."

I took what he said to heart. "My People" was then, and still is, one of my favorite poems. I feel I have covered the strength, the tenderness, the glory, the truth as well as an ideology that we as a people should work toward.

—AO

MY PEOPLE

My people are Black, beige, yellow
Brown and beautiful
A garden of life
with a love as sweet as scuppernong wine
growing in muddy waters
making brown babies
with pink feet and quick minds
My people warm sometimes hot
always cool always together
My people let's be together
understand that we've lived together
understand that we've died together
understand my brother that I've
smelled your piss in my hallway
and it smells just like mine
understand that I love your woman
my sister and her rare beauty
is reason enough for a revolution
yes sister my honest sister
I have had ugly moments with you
but you are the only beauty I've ever known
Yes sister my honest sister
you are the joy in my smile
you are the reality of my dreams
you are the only sister I have
and I need you
I need you to feed the children
of our race

I need you to feed the lovers of our race
I need you to be the summer of my winters
I need you because
you are the natural life in the living
at night there is a moon
to make the Blackness be felt
I am that Blackness
filling up the world
with my soul
and the world knows me
You are that moon
my moon Goddess
shining down light
on my Black face
that fills the universe
My moon I am your sun
and I shall take this peace
of light and build a world
for you my sister
Sometimes the waters are rough
and the hungry tide swallows the shore
washing away all memories
of children's footsteps
playing in the sand
where is the world I promised my son?
must he push back the tide
and build the world
that I have rapped about
Am I so godly until I forget
what a man is?
Am I so right until
there is no room for patience

My brother Oh my brother
father of a son
father of a warrior
My brother the sun
My brother the warrior
Be the beginning and the end
for my sister
Be the revolution for our world
turn yourself into yourself
and then onto this disordered world
and arrange the laughter for joy
the tears for sorrow
Turn purple pants, alligator shoes,
leather jackets, brown boots,
polka dot ties, silk suits,
Turn miniskirts, false eyelashes,
red wigs, afro wigs, Easter bonnets,
bellbottoms turn this confusion
into Unity Unity
so that the sun will follow
our footsteps in the day
so that the moon will glow
in our living rooms at night
so that food, clothing, and shelter
will be free
because we are born free
to have the world as our playground
My people.

NIGGERS R SCARED OF REVOLUTION

One day in the late spring of 1969, myself and Abiodun were sitting in Mount Morris Park, which had been renamed Marcus Garvey Park. Abiodun had just asked me what I had learned since I had been in Harlem. Without hesitation, I replied, "Niggers are scared of revolution." He countered, "Write about it, Umar."

"Niggers R Scared of Revolution" became a prayer, a call to arms, a spiritual pond to bathe and cleanse in. Because Niggers are not just vile and disgusting and shiftless. Niggers are human beings lost in someone else's system of values and morals. Niggers are dreams and hopes, pleading for fairness and a true sense of justice. Niggers find a safe place in their denial of just wanting to be loving and tender and kind.

—UBH

NIGGERS ARE SCARED OF REVOLUTION

Niggers are scared of revolution but niggers shouldn't be scared of revolution because revolution is nothing but change, and all niggers do is change. Niggers come in from work and change into pimping clothes to hit the streets to make some quick change. Niggers change their hair from black to red to blond and hope like hell their looks will change. Niggers kill other niggers just because one didn't receive the correct change. Niggers change from men to women from women to men.

Niggers change . . . change . . . change . . .

You hear niggers say things are changing, things are changing. Yeah . . . things are changing nigger things into Black nigger things Black nigger things that go through all kinds of changes. The change in the day that makes them rant and rave Black power! Black power! And that change that comes over them at night as they sigh and moan Oooooh white thighs. Oooooh white thighs. Niggers always going through bullshit changes. But when it comes for a real change Niggers are scared of revolution.

Niggers are actors. Niggers act like they're in a hurry to catch the first act of the Great White hope. Niggers try to act like Malcolm did but when the whiteman doesn't react toward them like he did Malcolm niggers want to act violently.

Niggers act so cool and slick causing white people to ask, What makes them niggers act like that? Niggers act like you ain't never seen nobody act before. But when it comes to acting out for revolutionary causes Niggers say . . . I can't dig them actions. Niggers are scared of Revolution. ·

Niggers are very untogether people. Niggers talk about getting high and riding around in Els. Niggers should get high and ride to hell. Niggers talk about pimping. Pimping yours pimping mine. Just to be pimping is a hell of a line.

Niggers talk about the mind. Talk about my mind stronger than yours. I got that bitch's mind uptight. Niggers don't know a damn thing about the mind or they'd be right. Niggers are scared of Revolution.

Niggers fuck. Niggers fuck fuck fuck. Niggers love the word fuck. They think they're fucking cute. They fuck you around. The first thing they say when they're mad is "fuck it." You play a little too much with them they say "fuck you." Try to be nice to them they fuck you over. When it's time to TCB niggers are somewhere fucking. Niggers don't realize while they're doing all this fucking they're getting fucked around. But when they do realize it's too late, so all niggers do is just get fucked . . . up!

Niggers talk about fucking . . . Fucking that . . . Fucking this . . . Fucking yours . . . Fucking my sis. Not knowing what they fucking for. Ain't fucking for love and appreciation. Just fucking to be fucking. Niggers fuck white thighs, brown thighs, yellow thighs. Niggers fuck ankles when they run out of thighs. Niggers fuck Sally Linda and Sue. And if you don't watch out niggers will fuck you . . .

Niggers would fuck fuck if it could be fucked. But when it comes to fucking for revolutionary causes Niggers say FUCK! . . . revolution. Niggers are scared of revolution.

Niggers are players. Niggers play football baseball and basketball while the whiteman is cutting off their balls. When a nigger's play ain't tight enough to play with Black thighs, niggers play with White thighs to see if they still got some play with. And when ain't no White thighs to play with, niggers play with themselves. Niggers will tell you they're ready to be liberated but when you say let's go take our liberation. Niggers reply . . . Oh . . . I was just playing. Niggers are playing with revolution and losing. Niggers are scared of revolution.

Niggers do a lot of shooting. Niggers shoot off at the mouth. Niggers shoot pool. Niggers cut around the corners and shoot down the street. Niggers shoot craps. Niggers shoot sharp glances at white women.

Niggers shoot dope into their arms. Niggers shoot guns and rifles on New Year's Eve a New Year that is coming in where white police will do more shooting at them. Where are niggers when the revolution needs some shot? Yeah . . . you know, niggers are somewhere shooting the shit. Niggers are scared of revolution.

.

Niggers are lovers. Niggers are lovers. Niggers love to see Clark Gable make love to Marilyn Monroe. Niggers love to see Tarzan fuck over the natives. Niggers love to hear the Lone Ranger yell Hi Ho . . . Silver. Niggers love commercials. Oh how niggers love commercials.

You can take niggers out of the country but, you can't take the country out of niggers.

Niggers are lovers. Niggers love to hear Malcolm rap but they didn't love Malcolm. Niggers love everything but themselves. But I'm a lover too. Yeah . . . I love niggers because niggers are me. And I should only love that which is part of me. Love to see niggers go through changes. Love to see niggers act. Love to see niggers make them plays and shoot that shit. But there's one thing about niggers I do not love . . . Niggers Are Scared of Revolution!

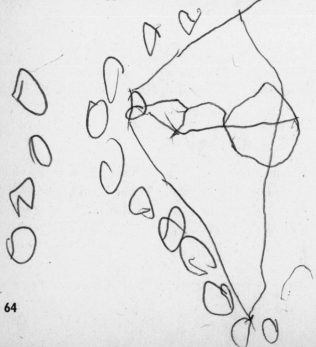

TALK SHOW

America sits a captive audience to the pain of its neighbors. Talk shows talk all day about pregnancy, poverty, perversion, abuse, addiction, and disease to millions of starving souls hungry to know that they are not alone. My whole life could be the topic of a talk show. They could do a week-long special on me, but I'm too proud to blast it in your face like that. Instead I blast it with my pen.

This poem was inspired by the women in my life. My grandmother was the first woman I fell in love with. Rose Fuller, my mother's mother, the "Captain," as she was affectionately called. Pretty black skin and Alabama-born. She was married at fifteen and the mother of fourteen children. She was the first real force in my life; the first strong person I knew. She kept me from going completely over the edge as a child. She took us in after my mother and father separated and we had nowhere else to go. It was the Captain who showed me what having a home meant and what it was to be in a family. She didn't completely change me, but she slowed me down some. My grandmother treated my mother harshly at times and I didn't understand why. This was her daughter, her own flesh and blood; as I got older, I realized that my grandmother knew that my mother was neither capable nor strong enough to take care of herself and her eight children.

So, very methodically, my grandmother went about teaching my mother to stand on her own two feet and become a responsible mother. I remember the time my grandmother found the gun and mask I was using during my kid stickup period. On the verge of tears, she kept asking me, "Is this what you're doing, boy? Is this what you're about? Is this what you want to be?" She was really hurt, that the demon had already settled in. My grandmother died from the complications of diabetes. She had gone blind, and she was totally dependent on others. I think that's what she died from: dependence.

My mother, Barbara, and I have always had a special relationship. She taught me how to read and how to use the language. It was she who would gather us all around and make us laugh to forget our hunger when there was no food to eat. It was she who came downstairs battered and bruised from being beaten all night by my father and iron our clothes, fix our breakfast, and send us off to school.

She was often tortured by her own family for having so many children and not being able to take care of them. And then people would insult and belittle her by asking if they could take this child or have that one. She gave up the oldest child, Larry, to my father's family and she regretted that decision her whole life.

Then there are the many mothers of my many children, Juwariya, Queenie, Malika, and Oni. Sometimes I was brutal. Sometimes I was warm. Sometimes I was inconsiderate. Sometimes I was very sensitive. Sometimes I was confused. Sometimes I made them happy. I always tried. The beauty of my experiences with these women are my children that came from them: Amina, Khadijah, Khalil, Sabriya, Aziza, and Issa.

My sister Sandra is the true legend of my family. She had a brain tumor in 1976. She was not expected to live. She willed herself to live and taught others to live in the process. She had her operation on May 23, 1976, and on June 28 she returned to work, weighing only 86 pounds.

In 1985 when I hit rock bottom and needed help, I called her in the middle of the night and she was at Port Authority within two hours to pick me up. I was so thin, she drove past me twice without recognizing me. My sister is a licensed nurse, but her greatest power is her belief in God. Her God Force. It is her God Force that rejuvenated the God Force in me. She showed me the little things again. Saying grace before a meal. Saying a prayer before starting my car. Thanking God for the blessings he has bestowed upon us.

These things made me realize where I came from and what drugs had taken away from me. I learned to laugh again with my sister. Sometimes we even laughed about things that were never funny. My sister told me that she came to New York to get me that late night at Port Authority because she had never forgotten what I had done for the family when I supported them as a shoeshine boy in Akron. I thank her for remembering, because they'd never put that part of my life on a talk show.

—UBH

TALK SHOW

Losing direction and then losing sight.
What starts out as love slowly becomes plight.

Seems so little when it's much too late.
Seems silly frustrations become silly little hate.

Lost in the memory of teenage grinds.
Seduced by illusion and then weaker minds.

Some have smiles and the gift for gab.
Some wait for the moment while others just grab.

Walking and listening to the falling rain.
Feeling that beauty and then feeling that pain.

Meeting halfway only to go it alone.
Waking up to the truth while asleep by the phone.

They change their minds hoping to change their ways.
Cocaine becomes a courtesy and then the ultimate phase.

Strained relations from casual sex.
A coin in the fountain while wondering who's next.

Crowded anticipation in singles bars.
Very slow time in very fast cars.

Short-term pregnancies with long-term ills.
Affection becomes a luxury and then it kills.

The children are hungry something must be done.
Turn a little trick and then have a little fun.

Open marriages with closed affections.
Secret rendezvous with midnight erections.

Emptiness and loneliness reflect in the dark.
Gang-raped in some well-lit park.

Silent screams and vicious sneers.
Assaulted repeatedly in their mother's tears.

Left to die in pools of blood.
Some perfect dream becomes some macho stud.

A fashion model with a radiant smile.
Concealing her darkness while exhibiting style.

Pole dancers with the greatest of ease.
Major intelligence becomes a minor striptease.

Pop singers. Soul singers. Fantasies galore.
Putting pain on hold while screaming for more.

Working girls. Sophisticates. Video queens.
All paying the price while stealing scenes.

Executives. Psychiatrists. Talk show hosts.
Handsome careers that become ugly ghosts.

Pornography is legitimized and then passed as art
For actresses who give up bodies for that special part.

Afraid to share. Afraid to give.
Afraid to love. Afraid to live.

The thought of suicide to end it all.
The prettiest smile at the debutante ball.

Crying at work. Crying to sleep.
Crying to go. Crying to keep.

Consoling each other while taking that chance.
A touch of sanity becomes a feel for romance.

To meet a moment just like you.
To need to know that love is true.
That feeling of oneness is so intense.
Some perfect example of common sense.

Feeling that difference but then feeling the same.
Wanting the prize but not the game.
Happiness becomes a simple goal,
to share each other and then the soul.

They take the initiative only to take the blame.
They take what is given but never the name.
They feed our hunger and clothe our despair.
They teach us to love when it's not even there.

Frequent encounters and one-night stands.
Rock stars without rock bands.
The other woman who has resigned herself to fate.
Who gets to swing on her emotions but not the garden gate.

By reasons of insanity they reluctantly cop their pleas,
as the logical conclusion keeps knocking them to their knees.
Mothers, lovers and very good friends.
Sisters who protect us and cover our sins.

Grandmothers before and then daughters who came after.
Who provide us sanctuary in their joy and laughter.
Patience is a virtue if you only give it time.
Why do we make them outlaws when there really is no crime?

Why do we try to deny them when we know we need them so?
Why do we try to ignore them but are afraid to let them go?
Keep the smiles so loving in the Summers of your face.
Forgive the bitter Winters so they never leave a trace.

Can you still feel the Spring before it just arrives?
Will you be able to support yourselves in the Autumn of your lives?

For when you learn to love yourself you will always be loved so
much. And here's one man who's not afraid to say, I cannot live with-
out your touch.

TO THE STREETS

The streets become your home away from home.

40 DEUCE STREET

My first piece of action was on Forty-second Street. I was a young Black man who had come to join the Black Revolution. I had given up my sharkskin and silk suits, lizard and alligator shoes, and most of my street ways. All I had with me was 22 cents, a book of poetry, and a pair of jeans I carried in a brown paper bag. Everywhere I looked there was potential for game and imagination. It was a virtual player's paradise. I loved it. Soon, I was spotted by a Jamaican who thought I looked just a little too country to be true. He tried running the Murphy game on me. But no sooner than he put that handkerchief and money in my hand and turned his head, I was GONE! The next thing I knew, I was hiding in this park on 43rd and Ninth Avenue and he was running past with this policeman, yelling "He went this away! They say, he went this away!" If I hadn't stopped myself from being totally seduced that first night on 40 Deuce Street, I probably would have lost everything.

Forty-second Street was a blur of faces, personalities, and characters. It was all shoves, pushes, and solicitations. It was the top of the world for me who had seen so much of its bottom. The more I came to 40 Deuce Street, the more I learned about human nature and myself. It was there that I learned about choices.

40 Deuce Street was a stage to act out your choices as well as a platform for their repercussions. It was a little bit of the village. A little bit of Harlem, a little bit of El Barrio, a little bit of Brooklyn, and a whole lot of loneliness.

This was the place to make your dreams come true at someone else's expense. 40 Deuce Street was my counsel, my friend, and my one and only true religious experience.

—UBH

40 DEUCE STREET

40 Deuce Street the weaver of magic.
Sometimes beauty. Sometimes tragic.

Where glamour and illusion are the welcome committee.
Where overindulgence becomes self-pity.

Where pleasure becomes the absence of time.
While dignity goes begging and confusion becomes Rhyme.

Where fresh young country boys courageous and bold leap from
Greyhound buses right into the fold.
While visions of promised land dance in their head,
Their dreams have already gone to join the dead.

Tears, sneers, and elegant queers all hung up in their lonely fears.
Whores bores and ashen-faced Moors all strung out in their midnight
chores.

I got that coke. "I got that smoke."
I got that feeling for a real good joke.
Laugh, giggles, and Midwestern grins
All dressed up for big city sins.

Games, hustles and
silk-laced schemes. Ideas, notions and arrested dreams. Where the
huddled masses yearn to be free. Where Hollywood pimps Miss
Liberty.

Which way is up?
reads a movie sign
where a nodding junkie stands in line
I got that Red! I got that Red!

Ain't got no place to lay my head.
A funky wino stands giving a lecture.
Partly reason, partly conjecture.
He says . . . to go down,
                    to go down,
to the depth of this pit.
Where you think you are but you're never it.

Where night survives at a fever's pitch.
Where the good die young while bastards get rich.

40 Deuce Street is nothing new.
It's always been there for me and you.
For people who seek that fast road to glory.
Who can open the book but can't read the story.

•

Where twilight pimps with manicured faces.
Share each other's social graces.
While living off of teenage girls with decorated smiles and gold
lamé curls.
Where natural beauties who once were pretty now try their hand at
being clever and witty.

He said, premeditated murderers of the highest degree.
Premeditated murderers of their own sanity.

It's where loneliness receives standing ovations. And starving poets
live off meager quotations.

The whole world is really a 40 Deuce where dreams are primed and
then turned loose.

It takes you over and turns you out.
Takes away reason and gives you doubt.

It makes you feel as big as life
as it cuts out your heart with a neon knife.

So vital, so young, so entertaining.
Faces so sunny but inside it's raining.

.

I got that GOLD! I got that GOLD!
Forty Deuce Street's got my SOUL!

Of all the negatives we can agree.
But there are some positives if you want to see.

It's where love is tenderly and tragically bound.
Where the warmth and softness can be truly profoun

Where the air is filled with a subtle romance
Waiting for the world to give it a chance.

Where many might dare to reach out and touch,
asking so little while giving so much.

Where a timid smile can warm your heart
Where relative unknowns get to play a part.

It's where life takes a strange and exotic form.
Where you try to be cold while praying to stay warm.

He said, we all seek acceptance to be understood.
Compassion for our faults respect for our good.
.

He said, my God, my God, I came so close.
Striking a sad and reminiscent pose.

He said, I almost had it in the palm of my hand,
until I took the life of another man.

He said, it was all over a hustle that we were in.
What made it so bad, he was my friend.

And as he sadly began to walk away.
He very wisely spoke to say
He said, never look until you can see complete.
For that is what I learned on 40 Deuce Street.

FUNK!

This poem got its beginning in the Bottom, in North Akron. The Bottom housed the projects and all the crazy and wild niggas. It was the Bottom of North Howard Street where all the bars and nightlife were. It was where Roxy's Cafe was and where I first came to understand Funk. Roxy's was always my last stop before I came home from shining shoes each night. On any night, you could open the door to go into Roxy's and somebody would be lying in the doorway, bleeding with the knife still stuck in them, and no one caring at all. Once you got in, Lawd have mercy, you couldn't believe your eyes. Men with patches over one eye, some with two. Women with no hair and all their front teeth knocked out. There were scars winding down the sides of faces, arms missing, fingers gone, legs lost. The average adult wouldn't even walk past Roxy's, let alone go in. Yet there I was, a nine-year-old man-

child in the midst of all this. Lawd have mercy. There was something that always drew me to Roxy's, even though grown people's blood was spilling all around me. I had to stop in Roxy's before I went home . . . to get some funk.

One night, I was shining a man's shoes and he was harassing a woman next to him. The woman kept asking him to leave her alone. He didn't. She asked again. He didn't. The next thing I knew, I was feeling drops of liquid on my head. I looked up to see where it was coming from. This woman had jumped up and slashed this man across the face with a straight razor.

—UBH

FUNK!

Up on the down, down on the beat
The funk of the slaveships become the sound in the street.

The funk in the strength in the funk of the weak.
The funk in the word when you decide to speak.

The funk in the sex when it turns to lust.
The funk in the ending when it turns to dust.

To master the Sun, to master the Moon.
Some funky little melody, some funky little tune.

The funk in the moment when it turns to love.
The funk in the push when it turns to shove.

Funky women with funky grinds.
Funky chaos in their funky minds.

Funky protection in funky scars.
Funky dances in funky bars.

I love you . . . I love your funk!
I love the midnight when it turns to Monk.

Funk in the morning with the blessings of God.
Funk in the logic that seems so odd.

Funk in the subtle secrets of night.
Funk in the wrong that wants to be right.

Funk in your dreams. Funky nightmares.
Funk in the children's terrified stares.

Playing in the music as it passes by.
Playing in that moment when it becomes a lie.

Can I be good? Can you be right?
Can this moment be kept in sight?

Seems so different. Seems so strange.
Seems so easy when it's hard to change.

Wrong directions and empty choices.
Outside the range of inner voices.
.

Insane! Profane! The brilliance of funk.

The sober thoughts of a funky drink.
That human element in the very least.
That funky moment that calms the beast.

Play that funk . . . Play it good.
From the boys in the band to the boys in the hood. Ohio Players
being true to the game. The Funkadelics and their funky name. The
funk being shared. The funk being real. The funk of the musicians in
the funk of their thrill. The funk of Memphis and the funky blues.
The funk in the rhythm while paying dues.

Relax with the funk, enjoy the ride.
The moment steps out and then inside. Funky Otis on the funky
dock. Funky moments on the face of the clock.

If you feel that scream . . . don't feel distant.
If you feel that moment make it instant.
Something so deep, so very inside.
Love so funky, it can't be denied.
Deep into the sound. Deep in the heart.
Deep in that moment when funk becomes art.

.

It keeps coming and coming always something new.
It keeps being tried while staying true.

Hazel, Hendrix, and James Brown.
Little Richard the funk of the town.
Bootsie Collins and his Rubber Band,
The funk in his mind becomes the funk of the land.

The O'Jays, the Dells so very funky.
Smokey and the miracle of Mickey's Monkey.

Funky little Prince in his funky little Ruse.
The Temptations stepping out in the funk of the muse.

Billie, Dinah, and the very sassy Ella, and Aretha so very classy.
Marvin on one of his funky trips.
The tears of his song on his funky lips.
Pain in the motions. Pain in the smile.
The funky gestures romance for a smile.
Caught up in his funk.
Caught up in his charm.
Caught up in his magic but not his alarm.

That funky thing at its very best. The ultimate pleasure and then the ultimate test. Here's to the funk that he shared so well. Here's to his paradise but not his hell.

Come dance with me on the face of the wind. Come feel my passion and by my friend.

Can I hold your hand when I need that walk?

Can I find you when I need to talk?

Can I feel the doubt and then feel the trust?

Can I feel I can't and then feel I must?

When you begin to feel that low. When you begin to think you've sunk. Just say the password to your self and quietly
dunk yo' FUNK!

BUM RUSH

They say that America eats its young. Well then, it completely ravages and devours its Black and young. You can't imagine what it's like being born in the inner cities of this country with a project as your reference point. You watch your brothers and sisters slowly fading into hopelessness. Basically, you see that all you have is the streets and a heart that must try to conquer them. And then people wonder why Black children have an attitude? Why are they so difficult? Why don't they trust anyone?

Who can they trust? Not long ago, a well-known Harlem minister decided to gather all of the Gangsta rap and hip-hop videos and steam-roll them to smithereens on the streets uptown. And we wonder why Black youth don't respect their elders? Instead of putting on this little political charade, the minister should have invited some rap

artists and their producers to his Church for an intelligent and respon-
sible discussion about the issues. These are our *children,* not some
alien forces that dropped in for a visit. These are our *children. If we
can't learn and don't learn how to talk* with *them soon, the chasm of
disrespect that exists now is going to get much deeper. I respect a lot of
these young people today. Not all of them, but some of them. I can
relate to and understand what they're going through. I wish the rest of
my generation could, they need us. These kids are just trying to do the
best they can . . . and what we've left them with, isn't much.*

—UBH

BUM RUSH

The Streets are calling.
The Streets are calling.

There's always the Streets. From shoeshine boys to big time to trick
or treat.

Trapped in the silence of primal screams,
abandoned buildings and part-time dreams.

The early signs become the later rage.
The latest death at an early age.

Young . . . bold . . . and unafraid.
Number one tunes on the hit parade.

Daddy came and then was gone
made a move that left a pawn.

Boys in the hood. Hoods on the head.
Living large to die instead.

They test the waters and dance the flames.
They hear the whispers but never their names.

Looking over shoulders to look ahead.
Overlooking paranoia to hear what's said.

The only enemy becomes the only friend.
The only way out becomes the only way in.

Indecent exposure to legendary fame.
Playing with stacked decks while destroying the game.

The divine becomes tempting and then cocaine
addiction becomes subtle and then profane.

Wearing the Streets like they wear a crown.
Wearing their dreams like they wear a frown.

I can't quit! I can't quit! This is all I've got.
There's plenty of drama but where is the plot?

Hey girlie, can you be mine?
Can I share this thought with you that needs to be kind?

If you take the cue, I'll take the chance.
If you'll be for real, I'll be romance.

Young boys . . . Young boys . . . skipping that rope.
Boxing with illusion while trying to cope!

The Pyramids. The Sphinx, and then Hollywood.
Miscellaneous. Miseducated and Misunderstood.

Consumed by power in the very least.
Consumed by greed and then the beast.

Every situation becomes someone to beat.
You feel the Devil's presence but you don't feel the heat.

Violence prone like blood to the heart.
Self-destruction becomes state of the art.

Riding in luxury with death on their minds.
Is it coming tomorrow, should I open the blinds?

Uzis, millimeters and Italian rags.
Gucci watches and body bags.
Designer jackets. Designer shoes.
Old-fashioned bullets with designer blues.

.

Passing time only to fail the test.
Down by law and then under arrest.

Play that music. Play it loud.
Take the fall and then play the crowd.

Wailing saxophones and funky base.
Same old cell block and C.O.'s face.

Using women like they don't exist.
Something in the mind begins to twist.

Gang bangs and free for all.
You stand erect but don't stand tall.

And mama with all her stress and strain and all . . . those prayers to
keep you sane.
Her voice that whispers in that time of night. Where human becomes
savage and blinded by light.

Where drug-related cops pick up drug-related dues.
Setting them up to be on the drug-related news.

Young boys. Young boys. You are not alone.
The dilemma is real but not your own.

The Streets take your soul and give nothing in return.
A point of reference should be a point to learn.

Nowhere to run. Nowhere to hide.
They become your excuse and then your pride.

Every little rhythm. Every little beat.
Every little thing becomes the Street.

Deeply wounded and deeply scarred.
You take what is left and you turn it hard.

You take the night and you make it day.
You take the consequence but forget to pay.

You take insanity and you make it sane.
You take the extreme and feed it your brain.

Thoughts are confused and then become odd.
Your slickness becomes arrogance and then your God.

Deeper and deeper into the dark abyss.
Drive by shootings that begin to miss.

Life becomes useless and carved in stone.
The Streets know the ending and set the tone.

Isolated from self. Isolated from mind.
Isolated from happiness you'll never find.

Love becomes instant and then a flash.
Misery becomes a nuisance and then a rash.

Peace of mind becomes distant and then far away.
Hope becomes a mute with nothing to say.

Emotions become callous and cold to the touch.
You want to laugh but it hurts so much.

You reach out to be touched but there's no one there.
You cry out to the streets but they don't care.

One morning they find you with your face in the mud.
There are no wounds. There is no blood.

But in your eyes is that mystery that has finally become known.
The streets don't work with anybody. They only work alone.

.

Young boys. Young boys. Don't make me repeat. The worst thing
to do is to die
in the
Streets . . . are calling. The Streets are calling. There's always the
Street.
From shoeshine boys to big time to trick or treat.

NEW YORK NEW YORK THE BIG APPLE

I had established a personal relationship with the naked city of New York. I couldn't imagine writing a poem about New York without cursing a little bit. The city is a curse. The intense gut reaction to this cold and callous dungeon, labeled trading post of the world is not soft lilac language. It's a curse. It's a pissy smelling homeless woman crouched in the corner of the Port Authority asking for some money. The only thing that disturbed me about this poem was I couldn't let my mother hear it. Foul language is something she doesn't tolerate. And, believe it or not, with all my revolutionary ways and postures, I never curse around my mother. Although this was written in 1968, New York hasn't changed a bit. Today, people just mistake her sickness for fashion.

—AO

NEW YORK NEW YORK THE BIG APPLE

New York New York the big apple
sixteen million feet nationals florsheims
thom mccanns stepping on each other
rejoicing over the death of one nigger toe
cold callous feet trodding up and down
synthetic avenues, streets, and gardens
gardens that grow shit
gardens where putty face beings sit
emotionlessly admiring bastard flowers
new york new york the big apple
new york is a prerequisite to america
a disguised sin
where some brother from that closed southern shit
comes to some open northern shit
for a vacation for an opportunity
that knocks up sisters and knocks him in the head
for an opportunity that takes him home with
dope in his arms and clairol on the brain
new york new york the big apple
new sameness new food same shit
new car same gas without platformate
new love same neurosis
new hairdos same minds
new styles same influence
new installations same holes
new words same story
new york new york the big apple
that empire outhouse

that receptacle for all varieties of puke
then there's queen liberty tin shit
standing in the middle of pee green water
telling a brother he's liberated
(the statue of liberty is a prostitute)
yes from the old mississippi to the new mississippi
new york new york the big apple
where freak looking filthy white rodents
are running around spreading new kinds of
venereal diseases talking about we love everybody
watching movies marked adult only
when it should be for kids only
the A train, the D train, the F train, the underground
undercurrent steel-plated frame
unworkable air vents ass aching benches and
then there's that corny paraphernalia all over
the interior inside of all of this there's a brother
being soaked in by that shit on the wall
suffocating from bad breath in the air
in pain because some jackass is riding on his foot
while on the train you see young and old white
wrinkly faces peaking over crooked shoulders
under cardboard hats poking their noses at you
vampire eyes staring at you wondering who you are
New York is an exploited colony called Brownsville
Bedford Stuyvesant or Harlem where tiny fat Jews
are holding the firey hoop watching you burn your
ass jumping through it
Er . . . . Siren sounds through the street
putting your mind in a state of mental paralysis
.

New York is brogan boot shape state
of Madison Ave negro button-downs
hungry lost nigger souls screaming
screaming downtown for death
semi-black obscured blackness
plastic trees and phony grass
New York is a state of mind that doesn't mind
fucking up a brother.

The Last Poets taking a break on the Lollapalooza Tour in Milwaukee, Wisconsin, 1994. (Courtesy of Carolyn Sachs)

To Ourselves

But my heart was big, my mind was quick, and my
spirit was willing. But more than anything,
I LOVED MY PEOPLE.

PERSONAL THINGS

*There was this bar I used to shine shoes in on Exchange Street. It was
a hillbilly bar. One day, while shining shoes, I met this little white girl.
She was about a year younger than me. I was eleven. She was in the
bar with her mother and father, who were both totally drunk. She told
me her name was Dora. I told her my name was Jerome. She asked me
to follow her outside. I said, "What about your parents?" She said,
"Let them sleep."*

*I followed her outside and into this little enclave behind the bar. I
never knew this little cubbyhole was there. I don't think anybody
knew but her. She told me it was where she came to be by herself. She
kissed me, as she began to take off her clothes. When she got fully
naked, she told me to take off my clothes. No problem. Then she said,
"Come here, I want to show you some candy." I went. This little white*

girl began to do things to my body that I didn't know a body was supposed to have done to it. How did she know all of this? Where did she learn it? This went on for about three or four Saturdays. Once, I even brought her flowers. We became friends. We talked to each other about our families, about how fucked up they were. We talked about all of our personal things.

One Saturday I went into the bar and she was sitting with her father in one booth. Her mother was across from them in the other booth, knocked out.

Her half-drunk father asked me to shine his shoes. I began. My eyes finally met Dora's. Her eyes were welling up with tears. I wondered why, but kept working. Then, I happened to look up under the table to see that her father had his hand in her panties. That is where she learned all that sexual stuff. She was trying to smile at me through her tears. I didn't want to see her pain. I finished her father's shoes, then I start walking away, but I had to look back. She had a smile on her face. I forced a smile, while walking out of the bar. I never went back to that bar again.

—UBH

PERSONAL THINGS

Time in becomes time out.
Group anxieties become personal doubt.

Expressing ourselves in dots dots and dashes.
Pure cocaine and false eyelashes.

Living inside words that seem to lie.
Living inside excuses that pass us by.
Living inside loneliness becomes a high.
Living gets mixed up with wanting to die.

A daily question of going insane while tormenting one another trying
to ease the strain.

Dreaming of tomorrows we'd like to know.
Repressing our thoughts while trying to grow.

The heart and soul are not involved.
Idle chatter becomes reality while problems go unsolved.

Prearranged. Prefabricated and preconditioned.
We're baptized, advertised, and posthumously mentioned.

Weaned and groomed for the glory of applause.
Living off the mercy of unwritten laws.

Shell-shocked patrons making peace with God,
While admiring the acrobatics of a junky's nod.

Turned into robots through the power of suggestion.
We seek an answer and become the question.

Afraid we might die before we live.
Blessed with life but then afraid to give.

We want to be amorous, glamorous, and larger than life.
Our cheap illusions become high-priced strife.

Losing ourselves in times of despair.
Becoming self-defeatists of unusual flair.

We rush toward the beginning that might be the end.
We sit in the darkness and try to pretend.

Pointing fingers while our insides bleed.
Committing suicide to fulfill a need.

Highly intelligent in a very low way.
We speak of existing but have nothing to say.

We.touch religion and make it seem like hell.
But then we touch unholy dreams and wish them well.

Faith is replaced with apathy and grief.
Indifference is made acceptable and then a belief.

Our left eyes all glitter while our right are blind.
We submit to this madness and hope it is kind.

Distraught women seeking compassion,
while turning tricks in high Roman fashion.

Finding love at the expense of losing their cool.
Looking for happiness but finding a fool.

Their moments of trust become deceitful charms.
One-night stands in strangers' arms.

Carousing with disaster in very high places,
while cutting off noses to spite their faces.

While the men play games of power and glory.
Tattered remnants of an old war story.

Outside themselves inside their heads,
top secret discussions on waterbeds.

Men without neither rhyme nor reason.
Lost in the depths of mental treason.

Abstract victims of the American dream.
Victims of a disguised but well-planned scheme.

Victims of a subtle but dangerous game.
Rugged individualism with a psychotic name.

We confuse the normal and exhort the extreme.
We make war a reality and call peace a dream.

American contradictions in Black and White.
We illuminate contradiction and call it the light.

America provides you with fortune and fame.
While stealing your soul for its own acclaim.

With the English language at its command.
It perpetuates illusion throughout the land.

Running big games in tiny print,
before you've got it, it's already spent.

Making sacrificial lambs of the Middle Class. Indulging in rhetoric
with its head up it lulls you to sleep with the six o'clock news and
then wakes you up and spoon-feeds you blues.

But from the darkness of ourselves we can find a brighter day.
Understanding and truth must show the way.

To understand that everyman's color will not be his heart.
To go inside yourself is where it must start.

To learn to be considerate. To learn to be humane.
To learn to use power and not become vain.

To understand you can be strong and not be crude.
You can be outspoken and not be rude.

To revile the tyrant. To protect the weak.
To insure the innocent their right to be meek.

To look on the sea and understand its motion.
To understand tenderness and give it devotion.

To understand courtesy and to make it a pact,
to understand what love is . . . and make it a fact!

Because we all must struggle. We all must try.
Because somewhere in the future we all must die.

But to leave a legacy that will long unfurl.
That ours too was a struggle for a better World.

25 YEARS

This poem was written on May 19, 1993. It is dedicated to a meeting that was held between myself, Abiodun, Felipe, and David Nelson. We got together to celebrate the twenty-fifth year of The Last Poets. Some of us hadn't seen each other in over twenty years. We talked about the past, the present, and hope for the future that all of those working or living under the banner The Last Poets *could come together and forget our differences and do something. After all, we have made significant contributions to American culture, recent history, and to the WORLD that have yet to be acknowledged. Are we bitter? Not me. I just keep doing it. I guess I would rather be a living legend than a dead one.*

Time and patience are on our side, I just wish we were. As you read this The Last Poets *are STILL going through changes. I'm a Last Poet and I know it. I own the name. I have the trademark to The Last Poets' name. I was the only one smart enough to even think about trademarking the name. Because if I had not done it, sooner or later somebody else would have. What really scares me is the fact that it may not have been one of the other Last Poets.*

—UBH

25 YEARS

The innocence of youth and age betrayed by the times we used to
dream of being men in movies and lies destroyed by our own passion
for the truth.

The same smiles and humor so sensitive to being cared for and loved
by those who say they understand.

This is no easy thing being the strength for the weakness and fear of
words lost in the dreams and nights of Harlem our inspiration to
leave and come back to in times of madness and coke and jail.

We love each other in the contempt for ourselves and what we have
to do.
No one has said it or done it better than us
you
me
we
are that last hope for those who cringe in the corners of themselves
and believe that there is no way out of the Projects and bitterness of
flirting with the edge and beautiful women and moments of peace
and substance abuse and the frustration of being
too good
too soon
too early.

Only we know what we have seen. Only we know what we have felt. Only we know what we have shared at the expense of being the warriors and lovers of the self-hatred and death that charm our hopes with cheap tricks of rehabilitation of promises too addicted to losing and quitting the game of being human and private confessions of just wanting to be who we are.

We are the friends to the tears that have nowhere to go. We are our fathers in that moment of night that speaks only to the softness of compassion. We are the doubt and hesitation on corners, in bars and in love with our people and being so much a part of their pain and laughter we sacrifice ourselves to the neon lights and being close to one another in the morning will come only when we learn how to control the darkness of ourselves . . .

THIS IS MADNESS

This poem had its beginning in the fall of 1970. I was twenty-one years old trying to live in Brooklyn on Clinton Avenue—455 Clinton Avenue, to be exact. The building was about to be abandoned. The owner was trying to turn it into a co-op. My older brother, Edmund Majur Watkins, and I were "liberating" one of the apartments, rent-free. Majur and I believed what we were doing was righteous because landlords and politicians in New York had gotten together and made living in New York almost an impossibility for the average man and woman. They raised rents astronomically, evicted innocent people, and strong-armed others into going condo or co-op. We were making a statement for the poor and disenfranchised whose rights are always toys for the rich and well-connected to make deals with in smoke-filled backrooms.

I was feeling very Islamic and gung-ho at this time. I belonged to the Dar-ul Islam Movement, Yasin Masjid on Herkimer Street in Brooklyn. And everybody knew about the brothers at Yasin Masjid, including the police and federal officials. We were known for our revolutionary fervor.

The Last Poets' first album had just hit the streets and was taking off! The next thing I knew, The Last Poets *had become a part of the national conscience. And as always, the nation rewards its famous with hanger-ons, and open-legged women with no panties on. Or there's jealousy, envy, rumors spread, and accusations. I then began to see it all clearly. It was madness.*

—UBH

THIS IS MADNESS!

All my dreams have been turned into psychedelic nightmares with
Rosemary's baby pissing in my face and Tiny Tim
sticking his moldy penis into my bleeding mind as it cries for the
strength to repel the sanctimonious sounds of the white rock group
the Grateful . . . DEAD! . . .
                                        are my aspirations
as they struggle for a free sweet smelling breath of life while being
choked by the Christianic gas passed by the Most Reverend Bishop J.
Fulton Sheen as he socks it to us
in the name of the Lord now . . .
And my realities have turned into a stone figuration of Miss Liberty
as she stands on the corners of the World selling herself to anyone
with the head of George Washington on them.
And all the while
he sits on a throne of Eagle shit with DDT in one hand and a White
tornado in the other wearing a crown of castrated Black Dicks while
reading the non-violent thoughts of Gandhi. And I watch him relax
by playing golf with Roy Wilkins' balls with Bayard Rustin glued to
his hand while xerox copies of Martin Luther King are popping from
his skull.
To dream the impossible dream.

Knock! Knock! Who's there?
It's Rap Brown and if you don't open up I'll strike and light and burn
your house down. And I see Malcolm's spirit his eyes burning Red
Black and Green flames and crying tears of thunderbird wine that

seem to touch my lips and make me thirsty for a taste of FREEDOM!
Freedom by any means necessary.
It's necessary to have freedom by any means necessary.
And I begin to hate with love and love with hate.
This Is Madness!
This Is Madness!
This Is Madness!

And I look up and see the moon bleeding lifeless white maggots and
screaming for my help as the Eagle's claws rip and tear at its virginal
form.

Oh Isis.
Oh Tuthmosis.
Oh Sun Ra.
Oh Allah.
Bismillahi Rahman Nir Raheem
give me your undying strength to rise up and reorder the Cosmos so
that man can truly understand and appreciate the Cosmic beauties
and realities of Science and Love. And he has turned the feminine
part of me into a sexual freak.

Look at her standing there in her micro-miniskirt made from the
strands of Freud's mother's pubic hairs and her uncovered breasts
dripping blood and pus and her lips colored with that anesthetic
white woman called Avon. But yet she smiles at me through the
indignity of Bull Conner ejaculating sperm into her mind and George
Wallace mentally finger fucking her at night in his wet dreams.
And her soft wet clinging tears of love seem to flood my heart with

strength to gather all my manhood from my heart with strength to gather all my manhood from my lower head and to put it back into my upper head.

And I hear my mother's voice rustling in the wind reminding me of the many times he tried to rape her of her Blackness. But she with the strength of a panther, the swiftness of a cheetah, and the cunning of a lioness would not be caged up with the other lies that kept me from being totally free. And when she came home at night I could smell the musty closeness of his body and see his translucent finger-prints on her tired weary physical structure depressed from warding off his beastly attacks.
But she would smile the smile of a thousand Black Orchids at me not realizing all the while that
the anger of a hundred lions was residing in my soul.

And during all this time my father was somewhere drowning his mutant plastic-minded self in a bottle of cheap wine letting that spiri-tual catalyst John Coltrane pay celestial homage to that White God who was riding his main vein.
This Is Madness!
This Is Madness!
This Is Madness!

And Diana Ross
how can you be Supreme and sing songs of Black Love when your mouth is overrunning with the Sperm of the trigger.
And William Styron is going to commit suicide when he finds out that Nat Turner made love to his great great grandmother. And he

has taken our most violent and militant leaders and stuck lollipops up their ass to pacify their Black power farts. And he is beginning to assume that all of us were born under the sign Taurus the Bull because all we do is BULLSHIT!

This Is Madness . . .
This Is Madness . . .
All this madness is madness . . .
Madness this is . . . Please stop all this Madness!
Please stop all this Madness
Please stop all this Madness . . . STOP!

LAST RITES

The Last Rites of The Last Poets must be a new beginning. When I stop and reflect, I realize that each of the Poets has been through something drastic in their lives—from mental institutions to prison, from college to drug rehab centers, from the armed forces to the streets to Europe and TV land—I'm clear about who and what we represent. We could never forget or forsake those brothers and sisters who affirmed our positions by their support and actions. We are still on a mission because the mission has not yet been fulfilled. There have been some battles won, but the war is far from over. "Last Rites" is the closing piece for the album Holy Terror. *My intent was to let the world know that The Last Poets in the nineties are reaffirming their purpose and fulfilling their responsibilities to themselves and the youth of today and their children.*

—AO

LAST RITES

And we shall live through
all the barrages of madness
that try to shoot us down
in living color
The Last Poets shall live
and grow stronger
with understanding
and grow wiser with love

For Nilija, for Miles and Monk
for Fannie and Sassy
for Mr. B and Dizzy
The Panthers and the Nation
We shall live in spite of ourselves
The Last Poets will rise
above the demise of all the lies
For our Mothers and their prayers
For your Fathers and their Dreams
For the passion in our lives
For the silence and our screams
For our Sisters and our Brothers
and all our children everywhere
and our friends

We can't win without our friends
and the last shall be first

and the first shall be last
We know the flow now
and hear our voices in the wind
the children are singing our songs
in the absence of a movement
they rebel among themselves
We will change that
we will be the light to
show them the way
we will be the fire for the torch
we will be the tidal of the wave
Ring the bell the shit is on
Daddy's Home.

To Our Ancestors

We know that our ancestors were the greatest
humanitarians in this world. We invite people into
our civilization.

DRUMS

*The first bembe I ever went to was in Brooklyn. It was the summer of
1970 and it was with Nilija, the original conga player of The Last Poets.
There was nothing like this in Akron, so I was very curious. As we
neared the building where the event was being held, you could feel the
drums and chanting and vibrating through the walls of the brownstone.
As soon as you came into the presence of the batas, the djembes, and
the shango drums your spirit was no longer yours. You were swept up in
a tide of awareness and consciousness that was so vibrant, so sensual,
so warm, and so very natural that you felt free. You felt honest. You felt
home. "Africa," "Alkebulan." "Cush." "Chem." "Ethiopia." All these
names were snapping off the fingertips of the drummers. All the power
of the ancestors was bright and clear and present.*

The thing that fascinated me most was the way the drums affected the women. They had a sexual connection to the drum. You could see their reverence, honor, and respect. These feelings were for the Gods and those who had come before them. This was for the future of their children who were waiting to come forth from the innermost recesses of their loins. The sisters went into a world of their own and the brothers respected that.

After that, I needed to know more about the drums. Nilija was a willing teacher. He was always ready to teach about the drums. Nilija was the heartbeat of The Last Poets. He was our soul and the revolutionary spirit we wanted more than anything.

—UBH

DRUMS

The Drums. So gospel. So Rhythm and Blues. The beat going in.
The beat going out. Dancing around the fire. A kind word. A touch
of Madness. The Drums. Always the Drums.

Trying to get out to sea. The laughter of idiots bleeding in my ears.
The echoes on land have become the insanity of charred and burning
flesh of children amusing illusion in the drunken and addicted
stupors we climb stairs to find ourselves in the pain of others.
No more lust.
No more pornographic decisions and business contracts in the
thrusts of darkened rooms and phony orgasms pretending to be you
are the man and I am the woman will you please take your
LONELINESS . . . out of me. I'm tired of playing this GAME!

The Drums. So gospel. So Rhythm and Blues. The beat going in.
The beat going out. Dancing around the fire. A kind word. A touch
of madness. The drums. Always the drums.

PANTHER

My first encounter with the Black Panther Party was by way of tele-vision. And for the first time in my life, television became real to me. I watched the Panthers march into the California legislature with their berets, black leather jackets, and GUNS! That shit blew my mind. Here was a group of young Black men doing what Malcolm had propagated: Defend your honor. Defend yourself. Defend your communities. I fell in love with these brothers instantly. Huey New-ton. Bobby Seale. Malcolm, Huey, and Bobby—that was my hall of heroes. Everybody always criticized the "street element" that existed within the Panthers, but that street element had to be there, for the heart and for the guts and for the courage to do and attempt to do what these brothers did. No educated, bourgeoisie Negro would have thought or even begun to think to do what these brothers did. No matter what you say about the Panthers. No matter how you judge them. Nobody can deny the fact that they made a whole lot of Black men, young and old, stand up much straighter and a whole lot stronger.

—UBH

PANTHER

The home of the Free. The land of the Brave.
Where fear and frustration dance on your grave.

Where Martial Law blows in the breeze.
Basketball players and the greatest of ease.

No more health care. No more dreams.
No more heroes. No more themes.

College education at a minimum wage.
Looking at the future and then turning the page.

Homeless in shelters. Homeless Tomorrow.
One paycheck away from homeless sorrow.

The Global economy becomes the Global slave.
Who do we dispose of and who do we save?

The Panther is yawning. The rhythm and blues.
Conservative smiles on the five o'clock news.

Here comes Newt. Here comes the ground.
Here comes the fury. Here comes the sound.

Hitmen for America with contracts to kill.
Right-wing fantasies on a Liberal thrill.

Debates. The deals and Media leaks.
They get the talk shows and we get the freaks.

Neighborhood jails for neighborhood crimes.
Family and friends drop neighborhood dimes.

No Public TV. No public opinion.
Total oppression over total dominion.

The real design. The ultimate plan.
Confusion becomes God and God becomes man.

Bobby Hutton was the first to go.
The Panther raged and tried to grow.
He licked his wounds. He buried his dead.
He bowed his arrogance.
But never his head . . .

Into the Country, out the back door.
CIA, DEA pimping this whore.
Guns, badges, and ID cards. Corruption complete with security guards.

A kilo, a vial, a pipe, a gram . . .
all closely related to Uncle Sam.
We sniff your bags. You sniff our blow.
Playing with justice while playing the pro.

Mom in the crack house, Daddy's at the border.
Dial 911 and place your order.
The war on drugs one great big joke.
Can you finish the paperwork while I finish the coke?

Record companies with thumbs up their ass.
Blowing smoke up yours while passing gas.
Sing that song. Tap your feet.
There goes our music here comes their beat.
It once was real. It once was true.
It once had meaning we once knew.

Powerful men with short little eyes, feasting on children with illusion
and lies. Control, manipulate. Manipulate control. They pump up the
volume and twist our soul.

Bunchy Carter was a sacrifice
while Fred Hampton paid the price.

They came from the heart. They came from the Street
without glock nines or hip-hop beats.

Gun battles, death, and mental fatigue. Who was down and who was
in league.
Gangsta rap. Gangsta sham. Gangsta dreams of who I am.

From the Rural South. The Industrial North.
The Panther came stalking, the Panther came forth.
Huey, Bobby, and Geronimo Pratt.
Afeni and Assata some of all of that.

Young, precocious, and very brave . . . They made mistakes but
always gave. Irresponsible, we sold them out. Instead of support we
gave them doubt. Afraid of ourselves. Afraid to be free. Afraid of
being what it means to be.

Niggas desiring the American prize,
trying Cointelpro on for size.

Turning their backs on the rising Sun.
Turning their backs to a loaded gun.
Caught in between what it means to be White.
The phony left and the dangerous right.
Protect yourself. Protect your kind.
Self-defense from a self-less mind.
Justice for yours, justice for all.

The beauty of the Panther up against the wall.
He wins. He loses. He fights again.
His love for freedom his only friend.
Understand the Panther. Understand the Law.

The fight for Justice can be brutal and raw.

MALCOLM

This poem came into being in the early part of 1991, while I was working on my solo album, Be Bop or Be Dead. *Bill Laswell, the producer, suggested that I add another piece to the album. At that time, I was living over Greenpoint Studio in Brooklyn. I went up to my room to begin the creative process. I thought about Malcolm. I tried thinking about how he would do this. "Keep it simple and plain, Umar," I heard him telling me. Not too many heavy images. No brain-racking metaphors. Tell what you loved about Malcolm. What connected him to you—that Midwestern Thang. What is it with the Midwest? Is it the air? Is it the music? Is it that good old midwestern work ethic? What did the heartland do to Charlie Parker? Miles Davis. Richard Pryor. Redd Foxx. Michael Jackson and so many others? What made them so innovative, unique, and revolutionary? What pushed them to want to sacrifice themselves and share their pathos, sensitivity, tears, laughter, doubts, fears with the world? I decided, they love the game. I thought of the players who were with Malcolm walking him to the Audubon Ballroom. They could feel the smile on his face when he saw the game going down. Glad that it was about to be over. Glad that his family could move on. He makes us so proud. A master player who faced death on his own terms. One who never faked the funk. One who never disgraced the game at anytime. We miss you, Malcolm Little.*

—UBH

MALCOLM

Midwestern images threatening the horizon.
Hold back the pain. Hold back the rejection.
I can . . . No you can't! I can! No you can't!
You're not supposed to. I will!

Going against the grain. Against all reason. Becoming an outlaw
very very young. Enjoying the status. The strength is the family.
My mother's tears become my beginning and my father's end.
Brothers and sisters become the inspiration for the poem
                    by any means necessary!
We will survive! I will keep the name high. They will respect my
mother. They will remember my father. I have the flag! I have the
flag! It did not touch the ground.

Learning the game. Loving the game. Obsessed by the game. And
then Harlem.
                    Harlem, the only game.
Neon lights reflecting the beauty of deep dark chocolate faces. Pretty
redbone legs and tight behinds. Very African and intimate suggestive
glances and invitations. Sumptuous lips full . . . of the reality for
every man's dream. Too much sensitivity for one highly sensitive man
to bare.
Loving the game.
Learning the game.
Obsessed by the game.
And then Harlem. Harlem, the only game.

Trying to be taught what you already know. Where you niggers been?
Y'all want game? Come to Red . . . and let's play! Play . . . Lady Day!
Play these streets like I was born in the middle of them.
Play Miles!
Play these women so hard so cold only to lose myself.
Play Bird!
Play with death like waking up so easy the next morning.
Game over.
Who won?
Ooooh, what is this?
cocaine.
White girls.
Cocaine.
Whitegirls.
cocaine.
There I go . . .
There I go . . .
There I go . . .

Harlem! I love it so much I hate it. It scares me. It fascinates me. It
enslaves us! In jail. Always in jail. Letters to my insanity. Memoirs so
intelligent, so brilliant, so deranged.
I think I'm sick.
I think I should get well. I think
I should
change.
So hard to stop the game. Revelations in the darkness of the pit.
Who are you? Who are you? The little lamb knows. My savior. He
tried. He believed. He was only human.
I love you Elijah Muhammad.

I forgive the envy. I forgive the jealousy. I forgive myself for believing in someone other than just Allah. They took my vision. But I still have my soul.

I've always had Betty. Transcending what it means to be man and woman. My joy was her smile. Her smile was my strength. In the worst of times she was that small little opening to the way out. She was that push forward to truth. She knows. She always knew. One pride and joy after the other.

Yes! He was my man. Yes . . . I loved him! These are the answers to all of the questions of what he meant to me. Amilah. Illyasah. Qubilah and Attilah my partner in crime.

Smile like your daddy girl! Think like your daddy girl! Be strong like your daddy girl!

Death is coming. It will come in Harlem. Where else? They want to humiliate me. To turn me into a joke. In front of my family. In front of my friends. In front of my true love. My one and only true love. My people. Forgive me Betty. Please forgive me. Dying in the sad memory of brothers eye to eye. Nose to nose. I respect you. You respect me. Let's go hunting brothers. Let's go hunting.

WARRIOR . . .

       who remembers that word, I do. I saw it smile at me in the face of death. Bullets . . . Bullets . . . Becoming part of me. Where is the pain? I love you brother. Self-hatred wrapped up in a twisted, demented but well-controlled smile. Where is the pain?

I love you brother.

All I have ever been was for all of you. Where is the pain?

I love you brother.

I have always loved you. I know that tune. I grew up with that tune. I love my people. I love my people. If they could just learn how to love themselves. They will respect my mother. They will remember my father.

I have the flag!

I have the flag!

It did not touch the ground.

INVOCATION

In the beginning was the word and the word was poetry and poetry was the light and the light was the way to a revolution. It was poetry that inspired The Last Poets and that caused them to be a fraternity committed to the revolution—culturally, politically, and spiritually. Bill Laswell asked me to write the opening for the album Holy Terror. *I thought it would be a great opportunity to clean up some of the conflicting tales about just who The Last Poets are.*

Even though there are conflicts that divided the group, neither the message nor the mission was forsaken. In an effort to unify the principles of the group as well as recognize and praise the worth of each individual member, I wrote "Invocation."

—AO

INVOCATION

And a South African poet named Kgositsile said:
"This wind you hear is the birth of memory"
When the moment hatches in time's womb
There will be no art talk
The only poem you will hear
Will be the spear point pivoted
In the punctured marrow of the villain
The timeless native son dancing like crazy
to the retrieved rhythms
of desire fading into memory
Therefore we are The Last Poets of the world
Said David Nelson, Gylan Kain,
Felipe Luciano, Umar Bin Hassan, Jalal Nuriddin,
Suliaman El Hadi, Abiodun Oyewole, and
the heartbeat Nilija (Obabi)
The Last Poets were born on May 19, 1968
In Mount Morris Park in Harlem, New York
It was a birthday celebration in memory
In honor of Malcolm X
The Last Poets were on a mission
We became the voices of the East Wind
Blowing away the West with our sound
The Last Poets, men who knew
In their youth the truth must be told
The lies must be revealed
And we got to be sassy and funky and sincere
about it
The Last Poets are individuals

Who don't flock together well
Who don't follow orders too much
And when we do there's a reason
When we infiltrate the madness
It's not for love;
Our lives are mirrors of the world
our people have lived and died in
For four hundred years
We, The Last Poets, are the seeds
For the rap artists to grow a garden
And yet we are only a branch
from the tree called Griot
Crossings is the road we've traveled
To come to this point
The Last Poets have become a fraternity
Of those who know
The mystery of a moon glow
And the wrath of each flame of the sun
The Last Poets are back
And that's a fact
No more time for bullshit raps
Let's get back on track

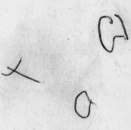

PELOURINHO

Brazil was a stop for the slave trade; Salvador Bahia was the major port that Africans from Benin and Nigeria were brought to and chained. While I was there with my good friend Ace, I had an opportunity to see and feel the torture and the madness. I was right there, in the square where it happened just a little more than a hundred years ago. Ace and I spent days checking out the square called Pelourinho, which translates as "a place of torture." When we were there, Pelourinho was filled with activity because it was Carnival time. The Carnival happens there and then religious ceremonies take place when Carnival is over. It was during our visit to Pelourinho that this poem started creating itself.

—AO

PELOURINHO

A blood line across the waters
From Benin to Salvador, Bahia
A scar across the face of the earth
Pelourinho
The place they brought the Africans
The place where they tried
To make them slaves
Pelourinho
You can feel the whip
Hear the cries
And see the blood in the red clay
The clay that holds the stones together
is African
And each stone is a bone
From a people called slaves
Pelourinho is the place
Where death came to dwell
His neighbors did not complain
For he was a way out
From the cold gray cobblestone streets
To the lifeless cathedrals
Tall walls of demons called angels
Haunted visions of white faces
Crucifying Jesus again and again
But'in the sacrifice of this blood
Of this dance with death
Comes life more rich
More pure

More alive
Where death spent
Many lonely nights
Pacing the floors of his funeral parlor
Waiting for someone to die
Pelourinho
A French word
Called a place of torture
Became a place of strength
A place where faces of white saints
Became faces of black Gods
Where haunted visions and demons
Became healing visionaries
And Orishas from the Motherland
And Jesus rejoined his kinfolk
And was reborn
And baptized in the sound
Of sensual skin tuned up
To dance to inspire
A fire like the sun
Pronouncing his presence
Pelourinho is the tongue of the flame
Licking the eyes of those
Who have tried to remain blind
Shining a light on a spirit
That would not be denied
No! The chains did not break
The spirit
Did not enslave the music
Of my soul
Did not shackle the will
Of my freedom

Did not tarnish the glow
Of my gold
And all the Pelourinhos
In Africa In Europe
In North and South America
Cannot destroy the majesty
Of my people the love of my people
Shining like the sun
Everywhere we go.

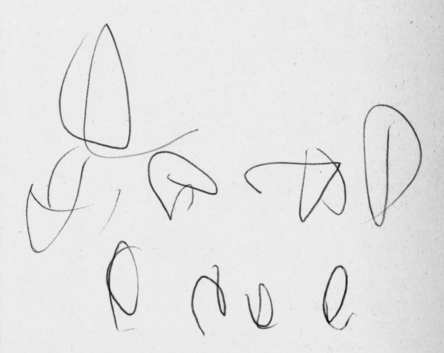

FOR THE MILLIONS

"For the Millions" was written long before I ever picked up my pen. My experience as an African American man made "For the Millions" my personal testimony. More specifically, "For the Millions" was inspired by the Million Man March.

James Mtume was asked to participate and asked me if The Last Poets would be interested in doing something with him. Of course we wanted to do something. We had thought just being there would be one of the greatest highlights of our lives, but to perform in front of a million brothers would be unforgettable in a few lifetimes. I thought, What do I want to say to a million brothers on a day of atonement? The word millions kept playing in my head. Finally, the title and *theme came all at once.* For the Millions. *I knew then that I'd talk about the millions who suffered before now and the millions who are still suffering, but also show the millions who have survived and risen above it all.*

—AO

FOR THE MILLIONS

For the millions of Africans
chained to the slave ships
For the millions of scars
on the Backs and Faces by the bullwhip
For the millions who jumped overboard
for the blood that poured
on the shores of North America
South America Central America Europe
and each ripple in the Ocean
is a grave for an African
who refused to be a slave
For the millions
who cut the cane picked the cotton
whose names have been forgotten
whose flesh has rotted
with the trees they hung us from
cut out the tongues
cut off our hands
if we played the Drums
For the millions
who were shot hung beat to death
tar and feathered boiled in oil
whiplashed backlashed
crocasacked and thrown in the river
castrated mis-educated segregated
integrated legislated by the constipated
For the millions who've been lied to

denied to vampire eyed to
misguided to and not abided to
So we decided to get together
and change the weather
not just for now but forever
we decided to love each other
Stop the madness
and be real sisters and brothers
we decided to stop and take a look
at the Beauty of ourselves
at this colored skin
and this thick hair
and these full lips
and this Africa all inside our Souls
still breathing the breath of Gods
in our lungs
Greatness is where we're coming from
For the millions who marched sang
prayed sat in laid in lived in jailed in
boycotted picketed spit at cursed at
yelled at like Blacks not where its at
like we should be satisfied
to ride in the back
for the Fanny Lou Hamers and the Rosa Parks
and the Eula Mae Johnsons and Harriet and
Sojourner and Eleanor Bumpers and
Assata Shakur and Gwendolyn Brooks
and the Martins and the Arthurs
and the Deacons the Panthers and James
and Langston and Richard Paul Malik
Marcus and Nat and Cinque and Kunta Kinte too

For the millions who know and those who have always known
that no matter what
"Truth crushed to the Earth shall rise again"
No matter how many bullets and prisons
diseases and deaths
no one can take our breath away
we are here to stay
no matter how much liquor and crack
nothing can kill the fact
that we are a divine creation
started civilizations
built the pyramids and the Sphinx
taught the world
how to pray and think
not to mention inventions
we never got credit for
and all the babies we raised
even when our own were ignored
For the millions with fire in their souls
that burns so bright
and the strength of our will
as dominant as the night
and the rhythm when we walk
and the rhythm when we talk
even when we have nothing to say
we utter sounds
that put color and spice in the day
For the millions
who are ready to turn this thing around
who are tired of being tired
and crawling on the ground
it's time to return

to our Spiritual Home
reclaim our Throne
and leave this American Nightmare
Alone.

Back row, second and third from left: producer Hank Shocklee and Chuck D of Public Enemy. Seated, Umar and Flavor Flav of Public Enemy. New York City, 1993. (Courtesy of Bill Adler)

To Our Children

You are your own person and I'm my own person
and I respect you and I want you to respect me. We
don't even have to talk about that, 'cause we just
doin' that. That just happens to be the way everything
is in this world. If it's going to survive.

TWO LITTLE BOYS

Sometime in the fall of 1968, I found inspiration while eating at
Sylvia's *soul food restaurant. I was sitting at one of the tables when
these two young boys came in. They couldn't have been older than
eleven or twelve. They were dressed rather shabbily, looking nervous
and apprehensive. They both ordered smothered chicken, cornbread,
collard greens, and potato salad. In only a few minutes they devoured
the food, looked suspiciously around, then bolted out the door. I was
surprised that no one ran after them. I thought to myself that they
were bold to do such a thing. Sylvia casually said to me, "I'm just glad
they got a hot meal."*

—AO

TWO LITTLE BOYS

Have you seen the skinny little boy
chasing the white ghost at night
face puffed up
tracks in his arm
and his mind blown
his mama's somewhere drinking
and talking about survival
Pops in jail
or downtown at the Y
the little boy chases white ghost
with his friend
and they get high
like cloud nine
where everything is fine
and no responsibility
have you seen two little boys
running past you with a lady's purse
they stole a black woman's purse
the other day yesterday today tomorrow
have you seen two little boys
eyes popping out of their skull
tracks in their arms
and their minds blown
talkin about trippin
talkin about flyin
talkin about gettin high
have you seen two little boys
sittin in Sylvia's

stuffin chicken and cornbread
down their tasteless mouths
trying to revive
a dying heart shrinking lungs
and a wasted mind
have you seen the sickness of our people
and all the while we parade around
in robes of our ancestors
and wisdoms of the universe
and all the while there are children dying
chasing the white ghost
whitey is dying
and his fucking ghost is killing us
Oh beautiful black hands
reach out and snatch the death
out of the youth
of our nation
Oh beautiful black minds
create a world
where children can play with life
not death
Oh beautiful black brothers and sisters
come together to create life
come together to create love
come together to create create
come together to create create
come together to create.

CRIME

I let these kids talk to me into doing this. I really didn't want to do it. I told them to do it without me. I told them they knew how to do it better than I did. I told them they had the skills and that I was just a poet. But they insisted. These young black and Latin kids in those brown khaki jumpsuits, residents of Spofford Juvenile Detention Center in the Bronx, demanded that I write a poem about crime.

Once I decided how I was going to do it, it almost wrote itself. I knew that it would have a much greater impact if written in the first person. People always want to hear your business. Even if it just sounds like yours. I also decided that my criminal would not remain tragic. He would evolve. Art must offer a light wherever possible.

Too many people think that young black men have criminal destinies. Crime is an industry, just like any other. Roles have been doled out. The crime game has been designated to the Black community. Be a cop or be stopped by a cop.

—AO

CRIME

Crime and doing time
It's a way of life
I got a gun and a knife
I'm gonna put an end
to all this strife

Take the money and run
I got my gun
hit the lady in the head
I hope she ain't dead
all I want is some cash
I ain't got no stash
I live from day to day
that's the only way
started back when I was three
nobody cared about me
My father did the bird
my mother never said a word
she just left me alone
it seemed I never had a Home

Now when I was six
I took a brick and stick
and broke a windowpane
the Super said I was insane
he said you should be put away

you startin trouble everyday
now when I went to school
the teacher said I was no fool
told my mother I was smart
but I had a broken heart
I needed someone to care
I needed love to share
Now when I was ten
I thought it was the end
my life had slipped away
where did it all begin
they put me in a place
where there was hardly no space
I started gettin mad
but I was really sad
thought I was gonna die
all I did was cry
it was truly a shame
and everybody was to blame
I didn't trust a soul
I lived in a dark hole
Hey whatcha gonna do
you know I got my crew
ice and dice nasty and mice
coolin out in my crib
on a ten to twenty bid
it seemed to be my destination
but I'll make it education
Turn the Force My Way
Put the Sun in My Day
Turn My Life Around
Put Back on My Crown

but all I can think of
is Someone to Love
Fill My Days and Nights
Let Me Know I'm Alright
Help me stop this crime
I don't need no more time
All I need is a sign
to Help me change my mind

Crime and doing time
It's a way of life
I got a gun and a knife I'm gonna put an end
to all this strife.

BLACK RAGE

When Bill Laswell said he wanted to produce a new Last Poets album, I immediately started thinking about themes I would like to address. Violence was at the top of the list. I knew I didn't want to just write a poem about violence. I wanted to describe a violent situation and expose all the implications. I also knew that I wanted to express that our children are not born with violence on their minds, but unfortunately in their quest to be men in this society, they are brainwashed to believe it's the only way.

—AO

BLACK RAGE

There are bombs standing
on the corners of the cities
waiting to explode
at the slightest touch
baggy shadow street boys
stand cocked ready to fire
their eyes are grenades
and the pin is about to be pulled
BOOM!
the Brother went off
pressure pulled the trigger
and the brother became a nigger
and no one could figure out
how it happened
what went wrong?
He had a chance
somebody even loved him
even told him that he was better
than most
but he went off
chains rattled inside his brain
and his sky was filled with clouds
that didn't even bring rain
but just the illusion
that something was coming
So he became a Gun
that he could hide in a jacket
and make believe he had an erection

all the time
he could penetrate anything
his tongue was a curse
his attitude was a bullet
and he'd shoot you down
without a second thought
He became G.I. Joe
killing his family
not the enemy
a human Gun made and manufactured
in the united snakes of america
There are bombs standing
on the corners of the cities
waiting to explode
at the slightest touch
baggy shadow street boys
stand cocked ready to fire
their eyes are grenades
They are warriors looking for
a Rite of Passage
They are young lions
enchanted by the sound of their roar
They are diamonds
treated like worthless stones
They are Rivers
with nowhere to run
They are dreams unfulfilled
desires buried in the remains
of an abandoned soul
they are the beauty of spring
blinded by the snow storms of winter
Soon they will see their Beauty

their Strength, their Love
and like the Rivers flow into sea
they will Unite as One
then our voice will be
more powerful than a Gun
and as we Speak
We'll get things Done.

MR. INTELLECTUAL

All those loans. All that time. All that reading. All that rote learning has to be justified. And whether it means anything or not, you will justify it. Four years. Six years. Eight years. Sometimes even twelve. Who are you without it? Where do you begin? What is Life all about? The sky is no longer Blue; it is open to discussion. You do not exist. You only think you exist. And we go on . . . and on . . . until the break of dawn. No matter how you try to shape it. No matter how you try to disguise it, you are now part of the distortion, the lie that lingers in the darker recesses of your consciousness. We have all the resources. We control all the means of survival. We are the masses. We are who "they" want us to be. We advertise them. We synchronize them. We even revolutionize them. We give them everything they need when we think it's necessary and when we think it's time. We are the educated.

We are the learned. The intelligentsia. We know everything, except how to satisfy our own sad, tragic, and lonely souls.

I've never liked the idea of higher education. Maybe it's because of one incident that sticks out sorely in my mind. It was on Wooster Avenue, the strip in Akron. I and a few of my homies were just kicking it on the Avenue. We were in our pinks, yellows, and blues and gators and lizards—just being the regular street people we were.

Up to the corner of Wooster and Raymond comes this British MG sportscar. It stopped at the light. Behind the wheel was a young Negro, or what is supposed to be a young Negro. He was dressed in a herringbone cap with matching jacket and the usual turtleneck. This Negro looked over at us with disdain and disgust that no cracker, no hillbilly, no white supremacist would have dared look at us with. We were the "niggers" who were stopping him from being fully accepted into the white world. As long as we were standing on corners, dressing and acting like we were, the white man could always point to us as the last little flaw in his character. This poem is dedicated to that young Negro.

—UBH

MR. INTELLECTUAL

So far away. So far inside. Running the show while trying to hide.
A degree in hand, illusion in mind. You think to bump and then to grind.
Lost in words. Lost in doubt. Lost in a moment that's left without.

You read the books, you pass the grade. You touch the light and then watch it fade.
So very simple, so very plain. You inspire intelligence and then bore the brain.
I wish you well, the very best. Don't take for granted while taking the test.
Here's to you and your very kind. Here's to that special confusion that's losing your MIND!

TO OUR WOMEN

Where do I begin? What do I say here? I don't want
to say I'm sorry. I've said that enough.

BLACK ROSE

*When I first started writing poetry, much of it was romantically
inspired. It felt natural to me to write about love and lust. However,
when I first started with The Last Poets I thought all my poetry had to
feel hard, like rocks being thrown at the system. Tenderness might have
been perceived as weakness, and I couldn't have that. Amiri Baraka
had written the classic Black love poem, entitled "Black Woman."
When he performed it, he'd have a group singing "Ooh, baby baby" in
the background. It was a sweet love poem, but it was strong, too. It was
the first time I'd ever heard love for a Black woman expressed like that.
I was touched and inspired to write my own.*

*Today, my two oldest sons, Pharoah and Obodele, have recited this
poem many times at school, in shows and to girlfriends. Presently, I*

use the poem in my workshops to point out that you don't have to be explicit to be sensual or sexual. I always highlight the line:

> I want to melt into your body
> and discover the base of your warmth

This takes us into a discussion about the power of poetry and how we can say less and entertain our imaginations more.

—AO

BLACK ROSE

She smiles and I smile
she walks no she glides
softly by me
changing night into day
She opens her mouth to speak
and Soul sounds
ring in my head
She speaks
and I want to dance
to her rhythm
She moves ever so gently
increasing my desires
desires to place my arms around her waist
and hold her close to me
I want to melt into her body
and discover the base of her warmth
Her beautiful Black body
that no human mind could ever conceive
She's love
She's truth
She's real
As real as the stars
that shine in the heavens
as real as the sun that bathes her body
as real as the moon that glows
and the birds that sing
and the rose that blossoms in spring
for she is that rose

but not just any rose
A black rose
that dwells on the hill
and looks at the world
A black rose
that stands as creator of nations
A black rose
A strong black rose
that never loses her petals
and blossoms all year round
Black rose
sweet rose
thornless rose
eternal rose
Please look my way.

LOVE . . .

This poem was created in the fall of 1986 in the town of Waterbury, Connecticut. The inspiration was a driving rainstorm. I had just gotten out of drug rehab in Danbury, Connecticut, and was looking for shelter in Waterbury to rest and plan my next moves. And everyone knows Waterbury is not the place to be stuck. They call the place "BURY." But that night a transformation took place. A very slow, gradual, and resourceful transformation. Here I was, standing in the rain, dried out, and writing about love.

Love was something I had denied so many others. And yet not knowing how much I was denying myself. What lesson was I supposed to learn this night? Why now? Why this town? Why in this condition? Love . . . what do you want from me? I asked, you've got to tell me now. "Love just smiled and answered, must I also tell you how?" The rain

173

felt soft and kind. An intense rush came over me. The words and images were coming so fast and so plentifully that they danced in the rain like little children. I began to memorize it right away. It was all so natural and so musical. When I was finished, I felt euphoric, relieved, justified. I stood there in the rain reading that poem to myself and anyone else who could hear me as they walked by. Finally I stopped. I looked around and realized that I was alone again with only my poem of love. However, despair didn't grip me as it had in the past. I found the strength to make my way to the shelter that night.

—UBH

LOVE . . .

Loving kisses and loving sighs.
To have love's pleasure bring tears to my eyes.

Love at first sight is so very rare.
Love may come late but it always comes fair.

Tears that humble. Tears that smile.
Tears that comfort and then beguile.

Where are the drugs? Where is the sex?
Where is the pleasure when there's nothing next?

Some love to love. Some love to hate.
Some find love but then it's too late

Games and lies where love should be.
Someone does it to you and then you do it to me.

Perversions, distortions inside the head.
When illusion dictates love is dead.

Love is not paranoia, love is not insecure.
When a man becomes a friend is when a woman becomes sure.

Love is the touch of a woman's hand
The respect for that touch is what makes a man.

The thought of love on its way to you.
The anticipation of what to do.

That funny little feeling that comes inside.
Emotions run wild but then try to hide.

Is he coming or is she not.
Affection needs tenderness and they both need a lot.

Why is it so hard to be at ease?
Why can't I be humble and just try to please.

Selfish desires that lead into doubt.
Sacrifice brings joy but love brings you out.

Soft morning clouds rush to cover the Moon,
like an orgasm with a future that comes too soon.

So when the thought of quitting begins to lose your mind,
put love before pain and leave the sorrow behind.

One night I was truly seeking, I was standing inside the rain.
As love passed by it whispered, time to leave the pain.

I'm here whenever you need me, I am the beckoning call.
I can be your rise to glory or the Madness before the fall.

I cried out, Love, what do you want from me? You've got to tell me
now. Love just smiled and answered, must I also tell you how.

To find that love again, the love you needed most,
the only friend you had when everyone was playing ghost.

Two star-crossed lovers caught up in that infamous strain.
Love becomes the struggle that tries to keep them sane.

In the glorious midst of nature, they try reaching out one night. She
learns how to kiss the darkness, he learns how to set his sight.

Love becomes the morning that shines so radiant and bright,
it becomes the hope and promise that once was a lonely night.

Where is that true beginning? Where has it all gone?
Why has love become a memory that just sadly lingers on.

Hard laughter disguising softer fears.
Love becomes entangled while deception cheers.

Love that moment you can't understand.
It's when love is asking for a helping hand.

Intelligence is vital, love takes reason.
Passion without wisdom is romantic treason.

Love is the rain that greens the leaves.
It's the part of death that never grieves.

The love of money can become the love of greed.
The love of denial can become the love of need.

Love is a woman so deep in thought.
A moment so precious it can't be bought.

That first kiss will always remain the same,
if not in principle at least in name.

Love is exciting. Love is bold.
Love grows gracefully but never grows old.

Love is being alone but never lonely.
It's yours truly and yours only.

It's when you think you should but you know you won't.
It's when they think you're convinced but then you don't.

Love plus patience can become understanding.
When love becomes too promiscuous it becomes too demanding.

Waiting on love can become the love of time.
Being impatient with love can lead to serious crime.

Love is to be considerate. Love is to be kind.
It's a wise old gesture from a childish mind.

To never take advantage. To never accuse.
To never mistrust. To never abuse.

Love is to be honored. Love is to be shared.
Love is to be tried but never dared.

Love is to desire. Love is to yearn.
To be able to give and ask for nothing in return.

And then to be able to speak words so true, I love you . . . and I love you, too!

VOWS

I'm okay, you're okay.

—UBH

VOWS

When the flowers have smiled their last smile and handshakes and congratulations hold on to one more dance in the corners of empty champagne bottles and loneliness catches the bridal bouquet in the middle of thoughts and doubts when I lay my body down next to yours exhausted from the fear of losing something very special to strangers friends all at the same time will tell if this is who we really are in the drama of coming attractions when we find it hard to express our feelings will you marry me in that moment of memories, pictures, and happiness when I forgot to ask you to please remember that I am only human.

When worldly affairs and your touch make me want to run and hide in winter storms and temptation and lust lie to love on silk sheets of denial and rejection and begging and pleading for your eyes to meet mine for some soft apology over impromptu lunches and long walks into empty arms and promising careers of pretending to be happy by the fire and pain holding up very well considering the fact that I find myself alone in the thought of some ridiculous smile and half-empty glass and bar stools and wondering why I can't humble myself to unconditional love and poems and prayers asking you to please remember that I am only human.

When I have found my way back to change and the courage to be a friend in your eyes will speak to me of the beauty of sacrifice and the humility of serving time waiting on one of us to be true to the words we spoke in the music, in the dancing on thin ice of wondering if you still care for me in this indecision of feelings and reason and dreams binding me to be there for you through all the confusion and hesitation of just wanting to let it be me for you in that moment when I close your eyes or you close mine, please remember that I always loved you.

GASH MAN

"Gash Man" is a pure example of using poetic license. I coined the expression one day while speaking with Amiri Baraka in Newark, New Jersey. We were sitting in my car having a "revolutionary" conversation, when this attractive sister strolled by. At the time, I was trying to explain something to Amiri when his eyes wandered off toward the sister. I noticed this and said "Hey man, you're not listening to me you're watching that sister. You're a Gash Man!" We laughed. Then he responded, "You better use that expression. If you don't, I will."

So, "Gash Man" was a new concept that in one word described a man who was "fucking just to be fucking, not fucking for love." Instead of the vagina being the entrance to heaven, it too often becomes a gash, an injury, a wound, as if a woman is being sliced open with a butcher knife and all that remains is a gash. Brothers who use their penises like butcher knives are Gash Men.

—AO

GASH MAN

Mm-m-m-m

Mm-m-m-m

It feels so good / Mm-m-m-m

And you tickle / And she swallows

Feeling good / So good

And those black thighs clapped up

Against one another

Like you weren't getting enough

It feels so good

Now there was pain / but it was good pain

Pain that hungered for more

And more . . . and more

And maybe tears or . . . Ummmm-ummm-mm

And you say take it easy baby / Take it easy baby

Good feelings (mm-m)

Flesh against flesh

And that hot moistness

That warm mucous

Surrounding your manhood / So good

Yeah it feels so damn good

Mm-m / The pain was there

But she said

(What did she say brothers?)

She said come on daddy / And you came

Everyday you came / You got beyond horny

You were now a gash man

Bleeding / and leaving a long stream of blood

From corner to corner / Stoop to stoop

Bed to Bed / And gash to gash
So good / mm-m-m
It feels so good
As sweat tickles down your back
With your revolution being dug
Out of your wax-filled ears
And your bleeding mind
Speaking strongly of death
And allowing blood to clot
And crust on the gash
Sing a song of evening time
Your days are numbered Mr. Gash Man
And all over bitches with big fros and nice bodies
Are turning would-be revolutionaries into
Gash men / Gash men
Same song yesterday / Same song yesterday
Gash needs man
No experience necessary
When you bleed to death Mr. Gash Man
And find yourself in a web of cold flames
And rotten watermelon rinds
And cigarette ashes and ashes
And byebyes and byebyes and byes
Don't forget your alligator shoes.

BROWN SUGAR

"Whore" "Bitch," "hoe," "slut," "chickenhead," "tackhead," "trick," and "freak." These are the words that many of our sisters are being called. I hear these words when I walk through the halls of junior high schools. I hear them on the train, on the street, in high schools, and, even worse, in elementary schools, too. It finally hit me when I was in Washington Irving High School running a creative writing workshop. I decided to make an assignment. I asked the students to write a poem using every positive word they've ever heard a woman called. The following week when I returned, the students had written some poems that many adults probably couldn't write. They used words like "my dear," "queen," "princess," "sister," "lady," "sister love," "my moon," "honey," "sweetheart," "lovely," etc. I did the assignment also. I thought it would be good for me.

—AO

186

BROWN SUGAR

Brown Sugar Honey Bun Lady Chocolate Supreme
You're the one that I see when I'm having a dream
I see you lying on the shore
By the water so blue
Even the waves applaud just because you are you
If I could be like the Sun
And touch your body and mind
I know our love would last
Until the end of time

But sometimes there is snow
And the water turns ice
For the warmth of your love
I know I must pay a price

Brown Sugar Honey Bun Lady Chocolate Supreme
You're the one that I see when I'm having a dream
Come sit under the Moon and let me sing you a song
About the world I will build
Where we both will belong
Once again I a King and you my Queen
And just like back in the days
We are a devastating team

Brown Sugar Honey Bun Lady Chocolate Supreme
Let me explain to you just how much your love means
There'd be no pyramids standing along the Nile
And gold would never shine if your face didn't smile
All the honey from the bees
Would be so bitter and dry
And all the flowers in the garden
Would just wither and die

It's the love that you carry in your body and soul
It's the wealth of your life
Much more precious than gold
I hope you see what I'm saying
Dig where I'm coming from
If you're not standing beside me
Then I can't see the Sun.

The Last Poets in Times Square, New York City, 1995. Left to right: Babatunde, Abiodun, Umar (Courtesy of Philip Greenberg)